鸣谢： LI KA SHING FOUNDATION
李嘉诚基金会

潮汕社会宗教与文化研究系列

处境与视野

潮汕中外交流的光影记忆

李榭熙
周翠珊 编著

生活·讀書·新知 三联书店

图书在版编目（CIP）数据

处境与视野：潮汕中外交流的光影记忆／（美）李榭熙，（美）周翠珊编著. —北京：生活·读书·新知三联书店，2017.9
（潮汕社会宗教与文化研究系列）
ISBN 978 - 7 - 108 - 06020 - 4

Ⅰ.①处…　Ⅱ.①李…②周…　Ⅲ.①潮汕地区-地方史-史料-摄影集
Ⅳ.① K296.52-64

中国版本图书馆 CIP 数据核字（2017）第 188158 号

责任编辑　徐国强
装帧设计　康　健
责任校对　曹忠苓
责任印制　徐　方
出版发行　生活·讀書·新知 三联书店
　　　　　（北京市东城区美术馆东街 22 号　100010）
网　　址　www.sdxjpc.com
图　　字　01-2017-7297
经　　销　新华书店
印　　刷　北京隆昌伟业印刷有限公司
版　　次　2017 年 9 月北京第 1 版
　　　　　2017 年 9 月北京第 1 次印刷
开　　本　790 毫米×1020 毫米　1/16　印张 17
字　　数　50 千字　图 231 幅
印　　数　0,001 - 7,000 册
定　　价　75.00 元
（印装查询：01064002715；邮购查询：01084010542）

总　序

　　中外文化交流与地方社会变迁，不仅仅是近代中国历史关注的课题，更是潮学研究的重要组成部分。第二次世界大战以后，随着历史人类学和社会文化理论在欧美学术界渐成风气，海内外汉学家亦尝试采取跨学科的角度，来重新审视潮汕历史社会文化的发展，通过几十年的研究，已经取得了辉煌的成就。

　　我们对潮汕区域历史、潮籍历史文化名人、潮人的海外拓殖史、潮汕区域政治经济状况、潮汕文化源流、潮汕方言、潮州音乐、潮州歌册、潮州戏剧、潮汕工艺农艺、潮州饮食文化等，都已有一定程度的把握。

　　潮学研究成果虽丰，在宗教研究方面，却未见相应之发展。当然，在潮学圈中，也有学者就潮汕地区各宗教的文化、历史及其与社会之互动等做了一些探索，例如对祠堂、庙宇、祖先崇拜、风水、亡斋风俗、宋代潮州佛教等的研究，又例如对潮汕地区的基督教传播、清末潮汕地区的基督教运动、20世纪教会办学的发展、汕头基督教教会的自立与分离、个别基督教宗派及差会的历史描述等的研究。然而，这方面的努力，至今仍然只属初探阶段，当中存在着不少有待填平的研究沟谷。

　　潮汕宗教文化也正是在这样的背景下进入了学者的研究视野。毫无疑间，潮汕历来都是信仰氛围浓厚的地方，其宗教文化源远流长、风格独特、多元而又开放，这既是潮汕文化的重要组成部分，也是海内外潮人凝聚乡族、延续传统的纽带。当把潮汕宗教放到中国宗教文化的大背景之中去考察时，也容易发现，它异常鲜明地体现了中华民族多元包容、融会贯通的信仰特点。

潮汕宗教的信仰风格，在它面对外来信仰时表现得尤为明显，潮汕基督教一百六十多年的发展历程，就是潮汕文化与基督教不断接触和对话的动态过程。早在 1860 年汕头开埠之前，基督教就已在潮汕本土传播，[1] 它与潮汕社会和谐并进，对牵动地方社会的现代化扮演了不可或缺的角色。[2] 潮汕地处沿海，自然灾害频繁，如 1911 年洪涝、1918 年地震和 1922 年台风期间，本土宗教团体及教会合力为救助灾民及灾后重建做了大量工作。[3] 同时，教会也对地方的经济发展有积极贡献，例如在 19 世纪与 20 世纪之交，于潮州商贸领域中举足轻重的抽纱工艺，正是由传教士引入的。[4] 另一方面，潮汕社会也以开放的态度接纳这种外来信仰，并以宗族为纽带，把基督教信仰

1　以往学界一般以瑞士巴色会传教士黎力基 1848 年在汕头澄海盐灶传教作为基督新教传入潮汕的开始，后经考证，1831 年及次年，传教士郭士立就已先后两次到过汕头南澳。胡卫清教授曾对近代潮汕地区基督教传播及发展的历程作过梳理，详见胡卫清：《苦难与信仰：近代潮汕基督徒的宗教经验》，北京：生活·读书·新知三联书店，2013 年，第 25—41 页。

2　如李期耀博士的研究就以美北浸信会（又称美北浸礼会）的教育、医疗、文字事业为考察对象，分析传教士及差传教会与本土社会的互动关系，以及其为潮汕社会所带来的积极影响；详见李期耀：《差传教会与中西互动——美北浸礼会华南差传教会研究（1858—1903）》，山东大学历史文化学院 2014 年博士论文。

3　相关研究成果如：Joseph Tse-Hei Lee（李榭熙），"Disaster Management and Christian Church Network in Early Twentieth-Century Chaoshan, South China"，*Berliner China-Hefte/Chinese History and Society*，35 (2009): 64-79。

4　相关研究成果如：蔡香玉：《坚忍与守望：近代韩江下游的福音姿娘》，北京：生活·读书·新知三联书店，2014 年，第 9—10 章；李金强：《福源潮汕泽香江：基督教潮人生命堂百年史述 1909—2009》，香港：商务印书馆，2009 年，第 49—51 页；李金强：《同乡、同业、同信仰——以"旅港潮人中华基督教会"为个案的研究 1923—1938》，载吴义雄主编：《地方社会文化与近代中西文化交流》，上海：上海人民出版社，2010 年，第 225—243 页。

代代相承；基督教信仰又与本土文化相结合，塑造了潮汕基督教的独特内涵，从而使潮汕基督宗教文化成为潮汕宗教文化不可缺少的组成部分；在广东省的基督教图谱中，潮汕地区基督教的堂点约占三分之一。[1]

以上这些因素也就是我们在 2012 年开始出版《潮汕社会宗教与文化研究系列》的原因。这套丛书广邀不同领域的潮学研究者参与，从历史、经济、建筑、艺术、文学、语言、民俗、中外交流、宗教对话等向度切入，发掘蕴藏于潮汕宗教文化中的人文宝藏，以多元的视野为深化潮学研究而贡献力量。经过五年的不懈努力，丛书已先后有六本著作问世，分别是：胡卫清著《苦难与信仰：近代潮汕基督徒的宗教经验》（2013 年）、林凯龙著《潮汕老厝：四海潮人的心灵故乡》（2013 年）、蔡香玉著《坚忍与守望：近代韩江下游的福音姿娘》（2014 年）、陈景熙等著《故土与他乡：槟城潮人社会研究》（2016 年）、黄挺著《中国与重洋：潮汕简史》（2017 年），以及李榭熙与周翠珊编著《处境与视野：潮汕中外交流的光影记忆》（2017 年），成果令人欣喜。

得蒙李嘉诚基金会的鼎力支持，并香港中文大学的大力合作，"汕头大学文学院基督教研究中心"于 2010 年初正式成立。中心以推动潮汕基督宗教研究、推广全人生命教育为宗旨，以多种面向、多种角度发展教育、科研及文化交流。在此基础上，为进一步拓宽学术视野、深化研究内涵，在 2017 年更名为"宗教文化研究中心"，致力于开拓多元宗教文化研究，计划就中国的宗教生态、中国宗教与传统文化、中国佛教的历史与文化、宗教慈善、犹太教文化研究等问题进行研究探讨。"面向汕头大学师生"是中心的根底，我们通过课程、讲座、出版等项目，丰富大学通识教育内涵，发展特色学术科研；"面向潮学及宗教文化研究学界"是中心的方向，为此我们不断深化与权威学术机构及学人的合作，搭建国际化研究平台，拓展潮学研究视野；"面向潮汕社会"则是中心的使命，我们也积

1 　2014 年 7 月 14 日，广东省基督教两会在揭阳市召开第二次潮汕四市教会联席会议，会议中指出：潮汕四市教会堂点 270 个，占广东省基督教堂点的 31%，并且潮汕籍教牧同工在广东省教牧同工中也占三分之一。

极展开文化保育，推动海内外潮人交流，致力于传承及弘扬潮汕文化。

丛书的面世，得到了生活·读书·新知三联书店的专业出版支持，我们深感荣幸。有各方的鼎力相助，我们深信，本套丛书能给海内外学者及读者带来一种人文新视野，并为推动潮汕地区的宗教文化研究及深化潮学研究做出贡献。

卢龙光

《潮汕社会宗教与文化研究系列》主编

General Preface

The dynamic process of Sino–Western cultural encounters has always been a major topic of research in the historiography of modern China and the field of Chaoshan studies. In recent decades, many Chinese and international experts have drawn on the analytical insights of historical anthropography and cultural studies to investigate the continuity and change in Chaoshan from an interdisciplinary perspective. Most of the scholarly works examine the Confucian transformation of the region, the role of prominent Chaozhou historical figures in imperial China, the opening of Shantou treaty port, the expansion of Chaozhou migrant networks in Southeast Asia, the development of Chaoshan dialect, and the varieties of local material culture, ranging from customary practices and opera to cuisine and handicrafts. Little attention, however, has been given to Chaoshan's diverse religious landscape, especially the resilience of popular religions and ritual customs, the spread of Christianity in the 19th century, and the changing relations between sacred and secular in the modern era.

Against this backdrop, this academic book series on "Chaoshan Society, Religion, and Culture" in was launched 2012 to advance a thorough understanding of the cultural heritage of Chaoshan in the early 21st century. The book series provide a valuable platform for Chinese and international researchers to explore and interpret the centrality of religion in Chaoshan from the past to the present. Our contributors draw on newly released archival materials, ethnographic data, and literary sources to evaluate the historical transformation of different religious traditions, ritual practices, and faith organizations in Chaoshan. Their writings reveal that the maritime society of Chaoshan has been characterized by a transnational movement involving local communities, international visitors, and faith groups in their joint efforts to build global ties and new hybrid identities. This process of cultural exchange gave rise to the Chaoshan spirit of maritime cosmopolitanism that was deeply rooted in contingent local conditions, and that continues to shape the meaning of Chaoshan identity today.

In the religious sphere, Chaoshan offers us a unique historical space where local and external actors met, accommodated, and engaged with one another. The Confucian, Buddhist, and Taoist transformation of Chaoshan greatly influenced the philosophical, spiritual, and ethical orientations of the local literati and lineage communities. From the 19th century onwards, the arrival of Christianity contributed to the larger project of modernization and the widespread embrace of modernity across Chaoshan. Shortly before the opening of Shantou as a treaty port in 1860, Christianity reached the coastal and inland areas of Chaoshan through overseas Chinese migrant networks and their native place ties. [1]The rural communities adopted and adapted the Christian gospel according to their preexisting values and norms. More importantly, Christianity played an indispensable role in advancing modern education, Western science and medicine, and popular literacy across the region. [2]In times of natural disasters and wars, the Christian missionary enterprises and local churches doubled up

---

1   Hu Weiqing, *Faith and Sufferings: The Religious Experience of Modern Chaoshan Christians* (Beijing: SDX Joint Publishing Company, 2013).

2   Li Qiyao, "Mission Church and Sino−Western Interaction: A Study on American Baptist Missionary Union Mission Churches in South China, 1858−1903", Doctoral dissertation, Shandong University, 2014.

their efforts to rescue local refugees and rebuild communities. [1] Furthermore, the Chaoshan churches directly contributed to the rapid development of embroidery industry in the early 20th century. [2] On the whole, people in Chaoshan were cosmopolitan and open-minded; they were willing to embrace Western ideas, technologies, and faith practices. As a result, Christianity became an integral part of the Chaoshan religious landscape and an important cultural marker of the local population. Today, the Christian population from Chaoshan make up a third of the total numbers of believers in Guangdong Province.

This book series has published six monographs on the religious, history and literary aspects of Chaoshan culture: Hu Weiqing, *Faith and Sufferings: The Religious Experience of Modern Chaoshan Christians* (2013); Lin Kailong, *Old Buildings in Chaoshan: The Ancestral Hometown of the Chaoshan People Worldwide* (2013); Cai Xiangyu, *Fortitude and Faith: The Female Christians in the Lower Han River Region in the Modern Era* (2014); Chen Jingxi, *Homeland and Foreign Soil: A Sociological Study of the Chaoshan People in Penang* (2016); Huang Ting, *The Central Plains and the Seas: A Brief History of Chaoshan Region* (2017); and Joseph Tse-Hei Lee and Christie Chui-Shan Chow, *Context and Horizon: Visualizing Chinese-Western Cultural Encounters in Chaoshan* (2017).

Thanks to the generosity of the Li Ka-Shing Foundation and the assistance of the Chinese University of Hong Kong, the Center for Christian Studies (CCS) of College of Liberal Arts at Shantou University was founded in 2010. Driven by the mission to promote a better understanding of the history of Christianity in Chaoshan and to advance the holistic life education among university students, CCS has developed numerous innovative education programs, comprehensive research

---

1   Joseph Tse-Hei Lee, "Disaster Management and Christian Church Network in Early Twentieth-Century Chaoshan, South China", *Berliner China-Hefte/Chinese History and Society* 35 (2009): 64-79.

2   Cai Xiangyu, *Fortitude and Faith: The Female Christians in the Lower Han River Region in the Modern Era* (Beijing: SDX Joint Publishing Company, 2014).

projects, and cross−cultural exchange initiatives. Based on this foundation, in order to widen up the horizon and deepen the research dimension, the center was renamed as the Center for Religious Culture Studies (CRCS). The new Center will devote itself to the discussions and studies of a variety of religions and cultures, specifically, in such fields as the religious ecology in China, Chinese religions and traditional culture, the history and culture of Chinese Buddhism, religious charity, and Judaism and Jewish culture, etc. Adhering to its mission "to serve STU faculty and students", the CRCS strives to be a key promoter of the liberal arts learning in Shantou and beyond. Setting out "to serve the larger communities of Chaoshan scholars who work on Chaoshan Religious Culture", the CRCS has built, expanded, and deepened intellectual ties with major academic institutions and scholars worldwide. All these efforts display our commitment toward globalizing the study of Chaoshan society, religion, and culture.

Finally, we appreciate the substantial support from the SDX Joint Publishing Company in Beijing. Our fruitful collaborations have not only made this book series a remarkably successful endeavor but also articulated a new humanistic vision for scholarly collaboration across disciplinary and geographical boundaries.

Lo Lung−Kwong, Editor−in−Chief of the

"Chaoshan Society, Religion, and Culture Book Series"

目 录

Table of Contents

序言一

　　学者追寻地方群体历史会面对两个挑战：一是在不存偏见之下，叙述历史人物的功过；二是如实地将史实资料呈现出来而不加修饰。对当代读者而言，他们读历史的目的，是希望看到个人经验和集体回忆的关联。而专业史家的职责，除了帮助读者了解和认同其研究结论之外，更希望启发读者培养批判精神，正如有句拉丁名言所说："历史好比一个有待开发和探索的陌生国度。"

　　李榭熙与周翠珊合著的这部潮汕历史影集，其挑战在于要跳出当代学人对宗教世俗化与政教冲突的框架，重构潮汕的宗教历史。这本书对潮汕基督教史的回顾，既中肯又全面；更重要的是，阅读本书使人享受了一次历史之旅，所见到的人情风貌、所感受到的精神氛围，都充满了基督教的烙印。年轻读者更能够通过这本影集与先贤建立关系，理解他们的宗教经验，从而加强对潮汕地区的文化归属感。

　　到底二人是如何通过本影集把严肃的史学批判与有趣的历史探索相结合的呢？他们大量引用了西方传教士的旧照，这些影像史料都完整地保留在美北浸信会和英国长老会的档案之中，其时间横跨清末与民国时期。这本作品的价值远超过一般搁在茶几一角的装饰艺术书。作者把影像置于特定的时空并加以诠释，让读者看到了一个在剧变中充满挑战与自由的潮汕社会。作者视医疗、教育、社会改良为现代化的柱石，把表面上看似"西化"的过程从现代化的大历史中独立揭示出来，并在潮汕地区这个层面上进行微观分析。阅读此书后，读者看待潮汕城市和海外潮人群体的眼光将会大不一样。

劳曼博士

英国伦敦大学东方及非洲研究学院

历史系高级讲师、《中亚学报》主编

Preface 1

The pursuit of communal history is challenged by two temptations: Firstly to express an implausibly unbalanced account of the community as historical hero (or victim), secondly to suppress information which could be construed as unwelcomed or even as embarrassing. The contemporary reader will try to establish a link, personal or by means of constructed collective memory, to the object of the historical study. The historian's task, in this respect, is to admonish the reader *not* to identify with the investigated matter, but to establish a critical distance. "The past is a different country" thus becomes Terra Incognita, a world to be discovered while reading one's way through a historical study.

In the case of Joseph Tse-Hei Lee and Christie Chui-Shan Chow's historical account of Chaozhou and Shantou, the challenge lies in recognising the region's Christian past without equating the challenges of today's world in general, and with those of the People's Republic of China in particular, with the complexities of the historical realities presented. And yet, this is more than a "critical reader" of the Chaozhou region's Christian past. The book is a thoroughly enjoyable excursion into a time when the identities of many of the families inhabiting today's Chaoshan, as well as the international Chaoshan community, were formed and given a distinctly Christian imprint. This book will therefore allow the young to reconnect with generations gone by, strengthening their sense of communal belonging.

How do the authors achieve the combination of "critical" and "enjoyable" in this volume? To start with, it is awash with missionary photographs taken in Chaozhou and Shantou. In their majority extracted from American Baptist and English Presbyterian archives, the pictures represent the entire time-span of the Republic of China (1912–1949), as well as several photographs from the late imperial period. But far from being a nostalgic "coffee-table volume", the present volume contextualises the images on display, thus creating a visual history of an extraordinarily agitated period, presenting unprecedented dangers, but also freedoms. Focusing on medicine, education and social reform as the pillars of modernisation, the image of "Westernisation" is being set apart from the larger process of a changing, modernising local society. Readers will never again look at the cities of Chaozhou and Shantou, as well as their global communities, in the same light!

Dr. Lars Peter Laamann

School of Oriental and African Studies (SOAS),

University of London, UK and Editor of *Central Asiatic Journal*

序言二

    当前中国各地纷纷出版如"老北京""老天津""老上海"等历史照片集，唯以传教士与中国民众的交流为影材者却不多。这本影集收录了两百多张美国浸信会与英国长老会在潮汕地区传教时的影像，并由李榭熙教授与周翠珊博士附以解说，它对于理解传教士与潮汕人民在日常生活上的正面交流颇具贡献。正如作者指出，影像史料背后所呈现的是一个中西双向的文化互动过程。照片凸显了近代中国从清末帝国体制过渡到现代民族国家的充满挑战的历程。然而作者强调，儒家文化与基督文明相互排斥的史观，并不适用于解释这个时期的历史巨变，因为图像记录了潮汕社会中，由传教士所带来的现代教育、西洋医学、灾荒管理和中西合璧的建筑美学。全书清楚地呈现了潮汕地区如何接受传教士的友善和他们的文化。对于潮汕社会在世纪性的现代化过程中与外来文化交融相汇的合作，本书提供了一个既权威又精彩的说明。

柯学斌博士
美国华盛顿州惠特沃斯大学
历史系教授兼东亚研究所主任

Preface 2

While China is now experiencing a dynamic interest in the collection and publication of historical photographs related to its past, such as photograph books on "Old Beijing (*lao Beijing*)", "Old Tianjin (*lao Tianjin*)", or "Old Shanghai (*lao Shanghai*)", relatively few books are being published on the important topic of Sino-Missionary encounter and exchange. This exceptional collection of more than 200 images related to the American Baptist and English Presbyterian missions at Chaoshan, by Joseph Tse-Hei Lee and Christie Chui-Shan Chow, represents an important contribution to our understanding of the positive diurnal relationships that developed between missionaries and local Chinese during the late Qing and Republican Era. As Lee and Chow astutely assert, "Underlying these photos is the remarkable process of cross-cultural adaptation". The images presented in this volume visually underscore China's challenging transition from traditional empire to modern nation-state and, as the authors point out, demonstrate that the hackneyed narrative of a "clash of Confucianism and Christianity" is no longer a sustainable view, given the contrary evidence of missionary photographs seen in works such as this. Observed in this book are stunning pictorial examples of missionary schools, the growing presence of Western medicine, missionary disaster relief, and the

处境与视野：潮汕中外交流的光影记忆

cross–fertilization of cultural aesthetic tastes in the construction of mission–related buildings that combine both Western and Chinese sensibilities. Woven throughout this work are illustrations of how Chaoshan natives embraced friendship and shared cultural space with the American and British missionaries. The narrative and photographs in Lee and Chow's book provides an authoritative and fascinating account of Chaoshan society in an era of cultural collaboration and modernization.

Dr. Anthony E. Clark

Whitworth University, US

序言三

    这本关于潮汕基督教群体的影集，生动地阐明了地方民众与西方传教士文化交流的活动。照片呈现了老百姓生活经历的真实面貌，从护理者背着病童走进诊疗室的一刻，到整个村子见证八旬归信者的浸礼，可以说这是一部介绍潮汕基督教群体生活之作。有些照片自然朴实——相中人不理会镜头而继续干活；有些照片认真严肃——相中人注视镜头，意识到自己的影像被捕捉下来的重要意义；有些照片仅仅呈现物质世界——山坡上的学生宿舍、被台风推到岸上的船只、方言写成的诗歌本，这些没有生命的事物，既展现了丰富多样的共同生活，又见证了冲破俗世阶层、自然灾害、语言障碍的毅力。

    书中影像与文字所介绍的潮汕基督徒，既有跨文化的世界观，同时又扎根于宗族、家系、村落。文化适应与相互感化是这个群体的特征。类似汕头福音医院的传教士机构，糅合了中西建筑的风格；在碑铭这类中国文化符号上，傲然引用《圣经》语句，借此宣告经文所界定的生命意义。

    本书指出了"文化帝国主义"理论对解释中国基督教历史的不足，潮汕人旺盛的海洋传统让他们倾向于追寻文化交流所带来的益处。在中西物质与文明相遇的过程中，潮汕人是居中调和者；对于远离故土为当地摆上生命的西来者，潮汕人为他们奉上热情的接待。

廖慧清博士

新西兰奥克兰大学亚洲研究学系讲师

Preface 3

    This book about Chinese Christian communities in Chaoshan vividly illustrates cross-cultural exchange between native Chinese and Western missionaries. The photographs show life as it was experienced, recorded, and represented by ordinary people. From a glimpse of a child on a caregiver's back stepping into a medical clinic, to a moment of community reflection at the baptism of an 82-year-old convert, this book interprets life within the Chaoshan Christian community. Some of these photographs are candid: the people in the frame pay no attention to the camera as they go about their daily business. Some are commemorative: the people look straight into the camera, self-conscious about the significance of their captured image. Some show only the physical and material world: school dormitories perched on a hillside, boats cast up by a typhoon, and hymnbooks in local dialect. These inanimate objects also display the rich texture of lives lived together, and a co-navigation of obstacles pertaining to class, natural forces, and language.

    The images and interpretations of this book show how the Chaoshan Christian community was both cosmopolitan and deeply rooted in local kinship, village, and lineage structures. This community was characterized by mutual cultural influence and adaptation. Missionary institutions like the Shantou

处境与视野：潮汕中外交流的光影记忆

Gospel Hospital displayed a mix of both Western and Chinese architectural elements. Chinese cultural symbols such as tomb inscriptions proudly drew on words from the Biblical text to proclaim the significance of the lives whose boundaries they marked.

The book's overarching thesis shows the limitations of the "cultural imperialism" interpretation of Chinese Christian history. It shows the people of Chaoshan, whose strong maritime tradition predisposed them to pursue the benefits of cultural exchange, as the "principal cultural mediators" in their encounter with Western material and cultural goods, and as accommodating hosts to transplanted Westerners who shared their lives.

Dr. Melissa Wei-Tsing Inouye

University of Auckland, New Zealand

序言四

　　自 19 世纪中期开埠通商，中国经历"数千年未有之变局"。后世史学家在试图了解这段中国邂逅世界的历史之时，目光经常驻足于上海、广州等通衢大邑。与此不同，《处境与视野：潮汕中外交流的光影记忆》一书独辟蹊径，将我们带到五岭以南、粤省东隅的潮汕地区。在乡土中国的广袤大地上，传教士与中国教会村落成为中西交流的纽带。教会在传统宗族势力的夹缝中生存并发展。新式学堂与宗教教育为中国地方百姓（特别是妇女）提供了新的知识平台，帮助他们探索中国传统之外的文化空间与信仰世界。教会积极参与并领导公益与慈善活动，成为地方社会治理中不可或缺的力量。我们要感谢李榭熙教授与周翠珊博士，他们慧眼独具，通过精心挑选与注解的黑白影像，让我们能够亲身领略一场信仰、知识、技术与权力的国际巡游，透过斑驳的历史遗存，开启尘封的历史记忆，找寻近代中国发展的曲折轨迹。

马钊博士

美国华盛顿大学圣路易斯分校

东亚研究系副教授、《二十世纪中国》副主编

Preface 4

At the dawn of the twentieth century, China found itself in the middle of sweeping changes. Foreign trade exploded, modern schools and hospitals opened, factories marked cities' emerging skyline, and churches reconfigured China's social and spiritual landscape. When historians attempt to trace the origins and outcomes of this global flow of people, technologies, goods, and ideas, they customarily lay their eyes on major metropolitan areas such as Shanghai and Guangzhou. But, *Context and Horizon: Visualizing Chinese-Western Cultural Encounters in Chaoshan*, takes a different and unique approach. It draws attention to the Chaozhou–Shantou area, a predominantly rural district located on the fringe of provincial administration and Confucian culture. It was precisely on the margin of China's political and cultural empire where a global encounter unfolded. Missionaries, both Catholic and Protestant, as well as the congregations of Chinese followers, were at the forefront. They appropriated the native lineage tradition and gentry domination to gain foothold on the local nexus of power. Christian schools promoted a curriculum of science and technology, which not only improved literacy but also offered many Chinese, especially women, new tools and frameworks to explore the world of knowledge. Foreign missionaries and Chinese church leaders initiated

　处境与视野：潮汕中外交流的光影记忆

and managed an array of public charity programs, from setting up hospitals to undertaking disaster relief. Chaoshan churches embodied a new range of administrative, informal, paternal and fraternal, and self−regulating patterns of authority. Their presence and growing prominence in local affairs altered the indigenous social and cultural orders. *Context and Horizon* reminds us that many Chaoshan Christians were quite cosmopolitan. They embraced new ideas and practices from the West, and they forged a form of partnership with foreigners to localize the modernizing experience. The partnership came under attack during the twentieth−century China's nationalist and communist revolutions, and a large part of such history is forgotten; but through well−chosen and carefully researched photos, Professors Joseph Tse−Hei Lee and Christie Chui−Shan Chow bring the memories of the localized global exchange to life.

Dr. Ma Zhao

Washington University at St. Louis, US

Associate Editor of *Twentieth−Century China*

序言五

　　文字记录并不能全面表达特定历史时空的复杂性。照片和影像却能呈现文字述说不了的信息，同时又能保留不断消逝的记忆，本影集正好说明了这一点。书中的人文景观，是一个多世纪之前英美传教士在粤东潮汕地区拍摄下来，并由本书作者附上文字解说的历史照片。比方说，照片记录了近代医疗与教育的设施，并提醒人们，外来传教士在改良地方社会和促进潮汕现代化上扮演了推动角色。当有关近代中国现代化的历史资料随着潮汕之后的巨变而急剧消逝时，传教士照片却像无声的证人，继续"诉说"宗教转化的本质力量。

　　这本书的影像史料，也显示了潮汕基督徒参与地方改良和近代化的积极作为。特别是相中的教会学校教师和福音医院的医护人员，他们说明了基督教教育和医疗事工中中西协作的历史意义。有关自然灾害的影像也反映了同样的精神。每当灾荒过后，传教士与信徒积极地与地方的商人和官员并肩合作，安慰灾民并解决他们的物质需要。最珍贵的照片莫过于那些平信徒、传道人和福音姿娘，他们充满自信的表情，证明了福音本土化的成功——若没有他们的参与，福音就不可能在中国土壤上生根成树。从中国教会史的角度而言，潮汕老照片指出，地方教会从一开始就积极追求和实践"三自"精神，这一点往往被学界所忽视。最后，本书照片凸显了潮汕基督教的特点，正如中国其他地区一样，传教运动是一个农村现象，这个基督教的乡土特质，也没有受到应有的关注。

　　随着时日推移，今天的读者很难明白潮汕先人如何生活，以及他们如何为求生存而战胜重重挑战。历史对我们而言恍如陌生的国度。书中的照片却为我们提供了19世纪中叶以来粤东社会遽变的诸多历史痕迹。正如作者解释的，我们是时候去摆脱传统的东方主义与西方文化侵略的视角，转而全面探讨基督教是如何与中国民间社会成功接轨的，就好像昔日潮汕信徒与传教士合作，成为中西文化交流的桥梁，让基督教会融入地方社会一样。本书是了解潮汕基督教历史的必读之作，因为当中的影像保存并强化了个人与集体的历史回忆，鼓励今日读者反思昔日信徒先贤的牺牲和贡献。他们当年的努力，有助于日后潮汕社会的蓬勃发展。

狄德满博士

英国伦敦大学东方及非洲研究学院历史系退休教授、

《近代中国基督教研究手册》第二卷主编

Preface 5

The written record cannot fully convey the complexities of particular historical situations. Pictures and images, on the other hand, can express many messages beyond words. At the same time, they make an important contribution to preserving the memory of an ever-receding past. This is particularly evident in the collection of photographs with explanatory texts depicting various landscapes and people in the Chaoshan region of eastern Guangdong in the late nineteenth and early twentieth centuries. The visual representations of modern educational and medical facilities are, for example, reminders of the Christian missionaries' contributions to the modernizing efforts a century or so ago. While much of the evidence of this past modernity has disappeared as a result of the dramatic changes in Chaoshan in recent times, these silent witnesses still "speak" to us with a powerful voice of the transformative nature of Christianity.

The visual material also indicates that indigenous Christians participated to a very significant extent in these processes. The pictures of Chinese teachers, doctors and nurses reveal the important legacy of the Christian educational and medical ministry in Chaoshan. Another feature of this close cooperation is demonstrated in the photos depicting the destructiveness of natural disasters. They remind us that in their aftermath foreign missionaries and Chinese

Christians worked closely with local merchants and officials in affording comfort to the bereaved and relief to the destitute. Probably the most precious images are those depicting ordinary believers, essential local preachers and ubiquitous Biblewomen. They highlight the key role of native agency without which successful evangelization would have been all but impossible. We can also conclude that the pursuit and implementation of the three−self ideal had progressed to a far greater extent than is acknowledged in the scholarly literature. Finally, these images throw light on Chaoshan Christianity—and the Christian religion elsewhere in China—as an overwhelmingly rural phenomenon. This important aspect has also been largely overlooked by modern scholarship.

With the passage of time, the modern observer cannot fully comprehend how people lived and overcame the many challenges in times gone by. For many of us, the past is indeed "a foreign country". These images provide vivid evidence for us to enrich and deepen our understanding of what really happened in eastern Guangdong since the middle of the nineteenth century. As the accompanying text makes clear, it is time to move on from the fashionable agenda of cultural imperialism and Orientalism and examine more comprehensively the relatively successful encounter between Christianity and Chinese society. It was the early Chaoshan Christians who, in partnership with the foreign missionaries, acted as cultural mediators and ensured the integration of the Protestant churches into the fabric of local society. This collection of photographs and images will, therefore, be of particular interest to the Christian communities in the Chaoshan region. The visual evidence in the volume will reinforce and preserve individual and collective historical memory and encourage the congregations to reflect on the sacrifices and contributions of their Christian ancestors. Without them the vibrant church life today would not be possible.

Dr. R. G. Tiedemann

School of Oriental and African Studies (SOAS), University of London, UK and

Editor of *Handbook of Christianity in China,* Vol.2:1800−Present (2010)

导　言

　　中外文化交流与地方社会变迁，既是近代中国历史关注的课题，更是潮学研究的重要组成部分。第二次世界大战以后，随着历史人类学和社会文化理论在中外学术界渐成风气，海内外汉学家亦尝试采取跨学科的角度，来重新审视潮汕历史社会文化的发展，通过几十年的研究，已经取得了辉煌的成就。

　　但从方法论而言，当代潮学研究仍要面对三个挑战：第一，由于学者关注政府如何向地方社会渗透与扩张，偏向于研究国家政权如何从上至下管理地方官民关系，这个研究视角基本上集中在国家的层面，忽略从地方社会角度由下至上探讨国家和社会的互动；第二，以地方的精英，例如士人、儒生、乡绅等为研究重心，对于宗族、寺庙、庙会和教会等民间组织在地域上的差异，以及形成背景、组成形式、运作过程和地方网络等各方面，皆缺乏深入的了解；第三，在研究民间宗教文化时，倾向于从功能主义角度来分析礼仪的政治和社会作用，忽略了宗教的文化影响力。

　　潮汕是一个文化和宗教多元的社会，其跨国移民网络更是 19 世纪初西方文明传入当地的直接平台。在鸦片战争之前，部分潮汕移民于东南亚接受西方文明，之后自发地回到家乡，标志着基督教在潮汕本土化的开始。当汕头在 1860 年开埠之后，大批欧美人士涌入，在当地办学，推动医疗和慈善事业，更发展了女学和抽纱工业，在推动地方社会现代化中扮演了不可或缺的角色。因此，研究西方文明元素在潮汕的中国化至为重要，因为这有助于读者全面地重构潮汕多彩多姿的历史，并向读者展现潮汕现代风貌和精神氛围内所满载的西方文化烙印。

这本历史影集诉说了近代潮汕地区的现代化经验，特别是当地与西方基督教文明相遇之下所呈现的影像资料。美国浸信会和英国长老会传教士的相机，平实而朴素地捕捉了西方物质文明和精神文明融入潮汕当地的点滴。当中的主角，既有不畏艰辛远渡而来的宗教人士、教师、医护人员，也有刻苦耐劳的潮汕先贤，他们的努力让西方文明落地生根，使之成为潮汕文化的一部分。几十年来的历史变迁，并没有完全磨灭西方现代化精神在潮汕地区的影响。今日潮汕人对外来的科学精神和技术文明的热切追求，与昔日对西方文明的开放态度一脉相承。在外来文明的熏陶下，文化传统与现代精神在潮汕有机地结合，启发潮汕人民追求科学观和实现中国梦。

和坊间不少潮汕旧影文献一样，本影集是早期潮汕开埠之后的重要记录。本影集有两大特色：

首先，它采取跨文化的视野，结合社会文化史学与影像人类学的方法，以相片中的人情风貌为切入点，力求再现西方文化与当地社会不同的互动，以及隐藏在相片背后的想象。

其次，这是传教士未曾公开的私人旧影的首次结集，除了一小部分已在美国南加州大学图书馆特藏部网站公开之外，书中所收录的两百多张黑白照片，都是英国长老会和美国浸信会传教士在 19 世纪末至 1949 年所拍摄的。在未公开的照片中，大部分浸信会的照片来自汕头大学基督教研究中心购于美国耶鲁大学神学院来华传教士的私人档案。另一部分浸信会照片收藏于美国俄勒冈大学图书馆特藏部，以及位于美国亚特兰大的美北浸信会历史学会。至于长老会的照片，其来源是英国伦敦大学东方及非洲研究学院图书馆档案室，以及苏格兰爱丁堡大学神学院世界基督教研究中心。第五章中有关盐灶、古溪、溪东教堂的照片是从教会文献中翻拍出来的；此外，其他彩色照片则来自李榭熙和汕头大学基督教研究中心韦红老师各自在田野调查时的记录。

正如在亚非拉地区一样，潮汕的传教士留下了大批宝贵的旧影，讲述他们与社会各阶层人士的往来。这些翔实的图片，凸显了中外宗教交流的长远意义和所形成的文化遗产。关于这方面的历史叙述，蔡香玉的研究是一例。她追溯了"汕头抽纱"事业的历史源流，反映了传教士带来的经济、物质文明，一方面促进了潮汕妇女手工业的发展，又为中国妇女制造了就业机会，提高了家庭的收入。另一例是关于潮汕近代方言与音乐文化的海外历史档案，包括现藏于英国伦敦大学东方及非洲研究学院和美国哈佛大学图书馆的《潮语圣经》、《客语圣经》、潮汕方言诗歌集、长老会牧师汲约翰编选的《潮正两音字集》，这些文献大部分都已被潮汕学者复制，现存放于汕头开埠文化陈列馆，让公众参阅。这些已公开的史料，说明了中外交流对潮汕普罗大众的文化提升，并对民间扫盲运动做出贡献。这些潮语诗歌集和《圣经》，至今仍广为海外潮汕侨胞使用，维系了普世潮人的身份认同，形成一个跨地域、跨时空的潮人文化印记。

本影集从宏观的角度让读者走进一段精彩的历史旅程，回到昔日一个极为国际化和多元化的潮汕社会。更重要的是，照片显示了外来文明进入潮汕的"多层次"面貌：文化传播、建筑美学、西学推广、施医赠药、赈灾施善各方面对社会所带来的新元素。地方上新生代宗教文化领袖的培育、结合中西建筑特色的教堂、西方现代教育中妇学和女学的感人故事、西方医学护理的普及化，都在照片中娓娓道来。

本影集的另一贡献是从微观社会史的角度，探究中外文化交流在潮汕的历史进程，其中以西方文化融入地方社会的本土化过程最为明显。自20世纪90年代以来，在对中外官方档案、传教机构档案、地方史料和宗教社会学的研究推动下，潮汕中外文化交流的历史研究取得了突破性进展。就研究的视野来看，潮汕学者尝试从西方天主教和基督教新教传教士建立的教会为切入点，研究信教民众在地方上的政治、社会和宗教活动，具体地探讨基督教群体兴起的过程，借此了解基督教在本土化过程中与地方社会的协调和冲突。尤其是胡卫清和蔡香玉的作品指出，潮汕基督教在不同的历史时段，皆积极参与并领导公益与慈善活动，成为地方社会管治中不可或缺的力量。此外，现代女子教育与医疗知识，又为地方百姓提供了新的知识平台，帮助他们探索信仰和追寻世界文化空间。

深受海洋文化孕育的潮汕社会，大大促进了中西之间的文化互动。环球的视野和地方的土壤，造就了其生机勃勃的文化内涵。潮汕先贤拥抱并使用近代知识、技术和处世方式去改善地方社会；西方传教士极力融入潮汕本地并以此为家。正当晚清社会仍然苦恼于是否进行现代化和拥抱现代性之际，潮汕先贤已经走在时代前沿，主动地与西方文化接触。这种开放包容的胸襟，正是海洋社会的特点，更是今日世代需要学习的历史智慧。

从方法论上讲，了解这些历史照片的使用背景和阅读对象至为重要。那些已经发表的传教士照片都被广泛引用。这些在旧时代发表的照片主要面向西方读者，寻求他们对传教事业的支持。这种实际的需要，往往影响到传教士对题材的选择。但传教士的私人档案中，还有无数没有面世的照片，这些照片往往保留了个人对传教地区的记忆、与个别信徒的友谊、对地方文化风俗的好奇，以及教会在建设基督化群体上所取得的成果。因而，每张照片不仅是一份独特的文献，它所涉及的题材广泛，所横跨的时段广阔，所记录的人情深厚，处处显示了摄影者在当地社会和教会情感上的高度投入。

使用传教士照片作为影像文献，有三种视野可供参考：第一种是"历史处境"视野。潮汕中外文化的交流是当地文明转化的行动，信徒与教会善用西方知识和资源去改善自身处境和建构新秩序，在动荡不安的19世纪末20世纪初找到新方向。照片所见的不仅是拍摄时的历史时空，照片本身更有其后续生命，正如美国密歇根大学的博士研究生贺威玮所言，传教士照片是维系中美民间交流的命脉，传教士把所拍下来的影像寄回故乡在亲友间传阅时，这些照片的生命就被延续下去，成为对遥远中国进行想象的素材。

第二种是"文化符号"视野。这个视野有助于跳出传统"文化侵略"与"东方主义"的狭隘角度，去理解摄影者与相中人的权力关系。人们常会忽略"拍照"可被相中人利用来向西方世界展示自我。正如香港中文大学彭丽君指出，近代中国照片显示了中国人不是无助的弱者；当他们面对象征强势西方文明的摄影者时，他们会把握相机快门被按下的一刻，以特别的姿态和眼神来表达自我。观赏照片时必须注意相中人的表情和身体语言，因为其所呈现出来的，可以是主人翁所构建的影像身份，它会远远超过摄影者的拍照初衷。传教士照片中的人物，不论是学生、医护人员、病人、女传道人、信徒、会众，抑或村民、路人等，并不都是站在镜头下等待传教士按下快门的被动者，而往往是向外界表现"我是谁"的能动者，让自己在相中的影像身份得以留存于世。

第三种是"草根社会"视野。"拍照"是 20 世纪初时尚但昂贵的活动，非一般人所能负担，只有商贾、官绅、名流才会拍家庭照和个人照。若不是传教士把镜头转向信徒、病人、孤儿、妇女、教会员工，普罗大众的生活面貌就会被遗忘。他们的照片为后世留下了重要的视角，对重构昔日民间社会的风貌提供了重要的证据。

本影集分成六个主题，分别是近代潮汕、办学兴才、施医赠药、赈灾施善、道在寻源和文化相融。每个主题的简介为读者提供最基本的背景资料。照片是本影集的主角，希望读者以上文所介绍的三个视野，在光与影、情与景、人与物的交融下，走一趟潮汕中外交流的历史之旅。

部分参考资料

蔡香玉著：《坚忍与守望：近代韩江下游的福音姿娘》，北京：生活·读书·新知三联书店，2014 年。

胡卫清著：《苦难与信仰：近代潮汕基督徒的宗教经验》，北京：生活·读书·新知三联书店，2013 年。

Ho, Joseph W. "Cameras and Conversion: Crossing Boundaries in American Catholic Missionary Experience and Photography in Modern China", *US Catholic Historian* 34, No.2（2016）: 93–106.

李榭熙著：《圣经与枪炮：基督教与潮州社会（1860—1900）》，北京：社会科学文献出版社，2010 年。

彭丽君著：《哈哈镜：中国视觉现代性》，上海：上海书店出版社，2013。

Introduction

This book is a captivating visual addition to the current study of Chaoshan society and culture. It offers a unique perspective on the symbiotic relationship between Christianity and modernization in Chaoshan. In particular, it focuses on the everyday experience of the industrious and entrepreneurial Chaoshan people through the lens of American Baptist and English Presbyterian missionaries.

Lavishly illustrated with over 200 black-and-white photographs taken by missionaries from the 1890s to 1940s, this collection of old photos takes readers on a fascinating historical journey towards an increasingly modernized Chaoshan society. It captures the ways in which the triad of Christian missionary movements—evangelization, Western-style education, and modern medicine—led to transformative social, cultural and economic changes.

Regarding the visual materials, most of the photographs taken by American Baptist missionaries were acquired by the Center for Christian Studies at Shantou University from Yale's Divinity School Library. Additional Baptist missionary photos discovered at the University of Oregon Libraries' Special Collections and University Archives in Eugene and at the American Baptist Historical Society in Atlanta. The English Presbyterian missionary photographs were found at the School of Oriental and African Studies Library, University of

London and the Centre for World Christianity at the University of Edinburgh.

As with other Christian missions in Asia, Africa and Latin America, the Chaoshan missionaries left behind many photos about their encounters with local inhabitants throughout the late nineteenth and twentieth centuries. Behind the photos are stories of the introduction of modern transportation, the use of Western curriculum in mission schools, the moving stories of women's education, the popularization of Western medicine in Christian hospitals, and the training of a new generation of cosmopolitan and competent leaders at all kinds of modern institutions.

Underlying these images is the remarkable process of cross-cultural adaptation. This two-way process took place on a global and local level. While the native Chaoshan people embraced and appropriated modern values, knowledge and norms to improve their ancestral homelands, Westerners adapted to the Chaoshan environment and made it their new home. As late imperial China had yet to come to terms with modernization (i.e., the process of being modern) and modernity (i.e., a sense of recognition that one situates at the most crucial juncture and the last point in a historical moment), the Chaoshan people were at the forefront of engaging the West. They took the initiative to foster mutual trust and respect with the outside world. This open and tolerant maritime culture is a lesson for us today.

Methodologically, understanding the background and experience of missionary-photographers is essential for interpreting their intention to produce these images. It is important to draw on three conceptual frameworks to examine the intersection between visual imagery and the human experience in Chaoshan.

First, the historical photos suggest that the Chinese-Christian encounters created a new civilizational paradigm that encouraged individuals and faith communities to construct a new sacred order capable of empowering themselves in times of chaos and confusion. Joseph W. Ho (2016), a specialist on the history of American missionary photography, urges scholars to investigate the immediate effects of missionaries' visual representations of their evangelistic experience and the "afterlives" of these pictures in the flow of information exchange and circulation between China and the US. On the one hand, the missionaries deployed photography to document their everyday life and to reprint the images for fundraising and other publicity purposes. On the other hand, the afterlives of the photographs enabled the missionaries to reflect on their deep emotions towards Chaoshan, and to archive the segments of their personal experiences and memories after many years of evangelistic service.

Second, the missionaries' photos challenge us to move beyond the dominant framework of cultural imperialism and Orientalism to problematize the missionaries' visual representations of the Chaoshan landscape and people. What scholars overlook is the possibility that many Chinese depicted in the images seized the photographic moment to assert themselves and access the outside world. Professor Pang Lai-Kwan of the Chinese University of Hong Kong states that the politics of photographic representations "concerns not the powerful West seeing the powerless China so much as the Chinese people seeing their new but fragile selves emerge in the face of a drastically new modern commodified environment, newly imported ideologies, and transformed everyday life" (2007: 3). This self-Orientalizing process was a deeply personal and public experience. It embodied a performative component in which the depicted Chinese appropriated the photographic moment to present their new visual selves to the outside world. This was particularly true for the missionaries who photographed ordinary congregants, mission school students, hospital staff and patients, and Biblewomen. They entered the missionaries' and their home supporters' visual imaginations with postures that transcended time and space. Therefore, photographic modernity should not be simplified as an imperialistic force imposed by the missionaries, but a dynamic instrument that shaped and democratized the Chinese-Christian encounters.

Third, the missionary albums fill an important gap in the scholarly database of visual materials on modern China. Many early twentieth-century Chinese photographers were deeply elitist and showed little interest in the masses. The photos contain rich visual materials about the commoners' daily experience and their responses to modernity. It was through these photos that the missionaries documented, came to terms with, and theorized Chinese everyday life as the site of an ongoing search for and struggle with modernization. The images of ordinary believers, refugees, orphans, Biblewomen, doctors, nurses, and mission school students draw attention to the embodiment of modernity and its liberating effects. New community governance and societal relationships emerged inside Shantou's Baptist and Presbyterian mission compounds. Intense social encounters between foreign missionaries and Chaoshan natives permitted a high level of accommodation, without domination and victimization. The core Christian values and norms not only became part of a Sinicized religion but also coexisted, intermingled, and fused with local Chaoshan culture into the maritime cosmopolitanism of the South China Sea.

All the visual materials are organized thematically in the next six chapters. Each chapter begins with a short narrative about the selected themes and topics. Chapter one looks at the foreigners' visual representations of the Chaoshan landscape. Chapter two revisits the history of modern mission boys' and girls' schools in Shantou, and chapter three focuses on the popularization of Western medicine. Chapter four shifts the focus of attention to several major natural disasters in the early twentieth century and contextualizes the Christian disaster relief efforts in a transnational context. Chapter five showcases the images of some church buildings and examines the fusion of Eastern and Western architectural styles. The concluding chapter returns to the larger issue of Chinese-Western cultural encounters and discusses the importance of these old photographs for historical understanding and heritage preservation.

In short, this book is more than a typical historical photograph collection. My photographic interpretation draws on the latest research in visual anthropology, historical analysis, and religious studies to reconstruct the indigenization of Christianity in modern Chaoshan. The goal is to move beyond the outdated characterization of Chinese–Christian encounters as the clash of Confucianism and Christianity. This idea of cultural clash has dominated the field of Western Sinology, and displays a tendency to portray the complicated process of cross–cultural interaction as either acceptance or rejection. The problem is that people beyond the margins of high culture were given no place at all within this framework. As we look at the old photographs, we can imagine what the missionary–photographers saw and heard, appreciating the rich history of modernization and cosmopolitanism in Chaoshan.

第一章　近代潮汕

在中国的地图上，潮汕似乎是一个偏远的地区。它位于广东省东北部，远离省府广州，在东北部与福建省相邻，在西北部则与江西省接壤，海岸线是连接潮汕与东南亚地区的唯一通道。潮汕地区还有很多纵横交错的小河、小溪和人工运河。潮语称这些水道为"溪"。1874—1919 年，活跃于此地的长老会传教士汲约翰注意到这样一个事实：许多村民都是沿溪而居，以便灌溉农作物。较大的乡村和集贸市镇，都是建于几个水流的交汇点，因为这样便利水上运输。在现代公路建成之前，溪流和运河是当地居民的经济命脉和运输干线。

1998 年，笔者在潮阳进行田野调查时，经常听到一句方言："喝哪条溪水，就讲哪种话。"这句话显示，溪流和运河是乡村之间势力范围的边界。"溪""河"是乡村的天然地标，是对土地和水源控制的记号，也是自我身份认同的符号。

过去的中国文人以大一统的中原内陆世界观，视潮汕为中华帝国统辖下的一个行政区域，并认为潮州府城在政治和文化上都要比潮汕腹地优越。这种看法迄今未变，甚至成为今天构建"潮学"和潮汕历史文化的一个关键要素。这种看法其实肇基于唐代韩愈（768—824）治潮的历史事件，表达了一种中原文人对南部地区的偏见。韩愈由于发表了反对唐代皇帝崇佛的言论而遭受惩罚，于 819 年被贬潮州。韩愈通过办学宣扬儒家道统思想和改变地方风俗，将潮汕纳为中华帝国的一部分。

由于韩愈治潮时推动儒学有功，故此后来的士人均奉他为宣扬儒家道统思想的先锋，将潮汕最大的一条河流命名为"韩江"以示纪念。这种将潮汕天然河道与国家符号拉上关系的做法，正好说明了只有通过"河""溪"这类文化符号才能帮助潮汕人理解以中原为本的儒学。

儒家文化框架只呈现出潮汕作为一个与中原儒家文化保持高度一致的地区，中国士人纯粹从儒家道统的角度审视潮汕地区，然而这个视角不一定反映当地的真实情况。西方则采取了一种迥然不同的视角。西方传教士和商人从南中国海踏上中国国土，完全是从海洋社会的角度感受和理解潮州地区的。

在逐渐熟悉了潮汕延绵的海岸线及大小岛屿之后，他们沿着韩江、榕江和练江向内陆航行，深入探索城镇和乡村市集。最明显的例子，是苏格兰长老会传教士李威廉牧师所绘制的传教区地图。李威廉在爱丁堡大学主修地理学，毕业后于1881年前往客家地区传教，他把地理学的知识应用到地图设计上。长老会于1857—1900年在潮汕沿海和内河沿岸建立了不少教堂，而李威廉所绘制的地图，都准确标示了每个教堂的位置和彼此间的距离，这清楚地反映了潮汕基督教的发展，是沿着海岸线和河溪向内地扩散的。

本章照片是传教士探访汕头市和内陆地区信徒时所拍摄的，照片显示了潮汕风貌的方方面面。传教士与当代人类学家最大的分别是，人类学家在田野逗留的时间相对短暂，而传教士则经年累月驻留一处，努力通晓当地方言与文化，融入地方社群，与社会各阶层进行交流，因此，他们所积累的影像资料相对深入而全面。此外，由于从事宗教活动的缘故，他们对一切信仰生活都颇感兴趣，这从他们镜头所呈现出来的民间信仰可见一斑。此外，传教士们也注意到潮汕地区现代化的过程，他们用镜头拍下了新型交通系统、汕头市内的现代化街道、商人频繁的贸易活动，这些都是西方现代文化从海洋世界进入潮汕地方后，为当地带来的变迁。

Chapter 1   Chaoshan Landscape

On the map of China, Chaozhou prefecture appears to be an isolated region. Located in northeastern Guangdong province and far away from Canton (Guangzhou), the provincial capital, Chaozhou is bounded by Fujian province in the northeast and Jiangxi province in the northwest. The coastline is the only corridor linking Chaozhou to Southeast Asia.

In addition, there are many small rivers, streams and canals cutting across the region. These waterways are pronounced in the Chaozhou dialect as *koi* and written in Chinese as *xi*. Many village settlements were built along the streams for irrigation purposes, a fact noticed by John Campbell Gibson, a Presbyterian ministerial missionary in Shantou from 1874 to 1919. Larger settlements and market towns were founded at the junctions of several streams because of the convenience of water transport. Before the construction of modern highways, streams and canals were the economic lifelines and transport routes for the local people.

Because farmlands were often located at a level lower than the rivers, the rural communities had to invest immense resources into digging canals and banking them to protect crops. Many villages used streams and canals as physical landmarks to justify their claim to the control of land and water resources. In the course of my fieldwork in Chaoyang district in 1998, I often heard locals say, "Whatever language you speak depends on which river water you drink". Underlying this saying is the idea that streams and canals are territorial boundaries between villages.

Chinese literati had long perceived Chaoshan as an administrative unit within the imperial empire, and assumed the political and cultural supremacy of the Chaozhou prefectural city over the hinterlands. The literati's perception of Chaoshan remained intact throughout the nineteenth century, and even constitutes a key element in the scholarly construction of Chaozhou today.

This bias is based on the Confucian transformation of the region by Han Yu (768–824) in the Tang dynasty. Han Yu, a well-known Tang scholar and poet, was sent in 819 to be the Chaozhou prefect as a punishment for his anti-Buddhist remarks against the Emperor. Later generations of scholars regarded Han Yu as the pioneer in propagating Confucian orthodoxy, and named the largest local river after him—the Han River.

Han Yu's pioneering was followed by a long period of Han Chinese cultural expansion into the area. Through the teaching of the Confucian classics, school construction, and reform of local customs, Chaoshan became integrated into the imperial empire. The literati portrayed Chaoshan as a highly unified and homogeneous region oriented towards the political center in the north, and tells us only about the Sinicization of Chaozhou, rather than its local reality.

While Chinese literati observed Chaozhou from the perspective of the Confucian imperial empire, Western observers adopted a completely different point of view. Arriving to the region from the South China Sea, Westerners perceived Chaozhou entirely from its coast and their own mission stations.

After familiarizing themselves with the long coastline, outlying islands, and sea ports, Westerners sailed along the Han, Rong and Lian rivers to explore market towns and villages in the interior. The best example of this is the map drawn by missionary Rev. William Riddel, who graduated with an M.A. in geography from the University of Edinburgh and came to work in the Hakka-speaking interior in 1881. His map not only reconstructs the geography of the Presbyterian missionary movement from a maritime perspective but also reveals that the center of Chaoshan Christianity was in the countryside, not in the treaty port of Shantou.

Most of the photographs in this chapter were taken by missionaries during their country tours. It is indeed impressive to see the wide range of images of the Chaoshan landscape. The conditions in which they produced these visual materials were different from the half-to-one-year field studies in which anthropologists observed and investigated the rituals performed by isolated communities. The missionaries were fluent in the Chaoshan dialect and spent decades living locally. As insightful ritual observers and dedicated religious workers, they acquired first-hand accounts of Chaoshan society and gathered many materials on local customs. The photos touch on issues arising from the challenges of evangelization in Chaoshan society, especially the missionaries' experience of cultural shock, communication difficulties, and the meaning of popular religious rituals. The rich ethnographic data extracted from these images highlight the fast-changing landscape of Chaoshan.

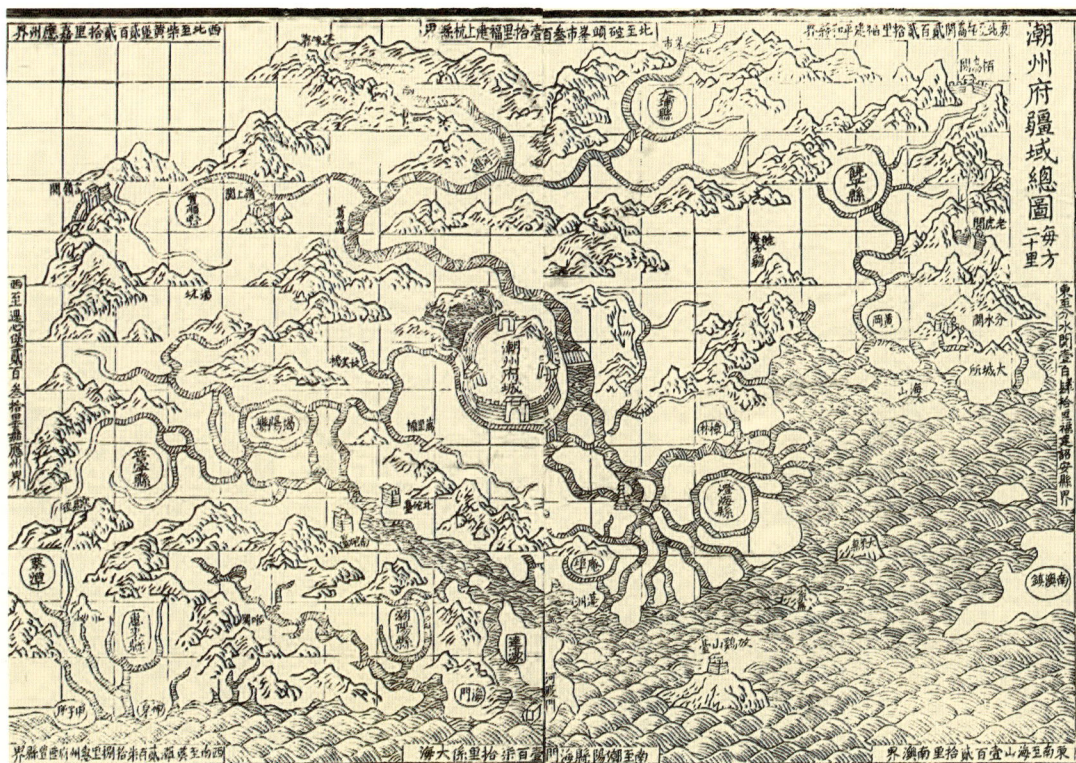

乾隆潮州府疆域总图
Chaozhou Prefecture

On trip to Pho Leng. Carman's "boy" o8o8
pressed the bulb before we were ready.
I was trying to make man sit down. Type
of river row boat, rowed before & aft.
Boat man in rear. Passenger compartment
under mat shed. Background, mts.& fields.
L o R bamboo, oranges, sugar cane, bamboo

美国浸信会的福音船。（教会所藏照片大多带有比例尺和简要说明，本图保留原貌，以下为了观赏效果予以裁切。）照片下方文字解释，其中一位传教士的少年仆人在船还没有泊岸就急于下船，传教士为安全起见，提醒大家要小心。又提到戴着草帽的船夫在船尾掌舵，而其他乘客则坐在由竹席搭建的船舱内，船头放满了橘子、甘蔗、竹竿等

The American Baptist missionaries traveled to Punning district by boat in 1922. A missionary's servant pressed the bulb before the boat reached the shore while Rev. Adam Groesbeck urged all passengers to sit down. This was a typical inland river rowing boat and everyone relied on it to visit the interior. The passenger compartment was placed under a mat shed, and the passengers carried baskets of oranges, bamboo and sugar cane. Orchids and rice fields were in the background

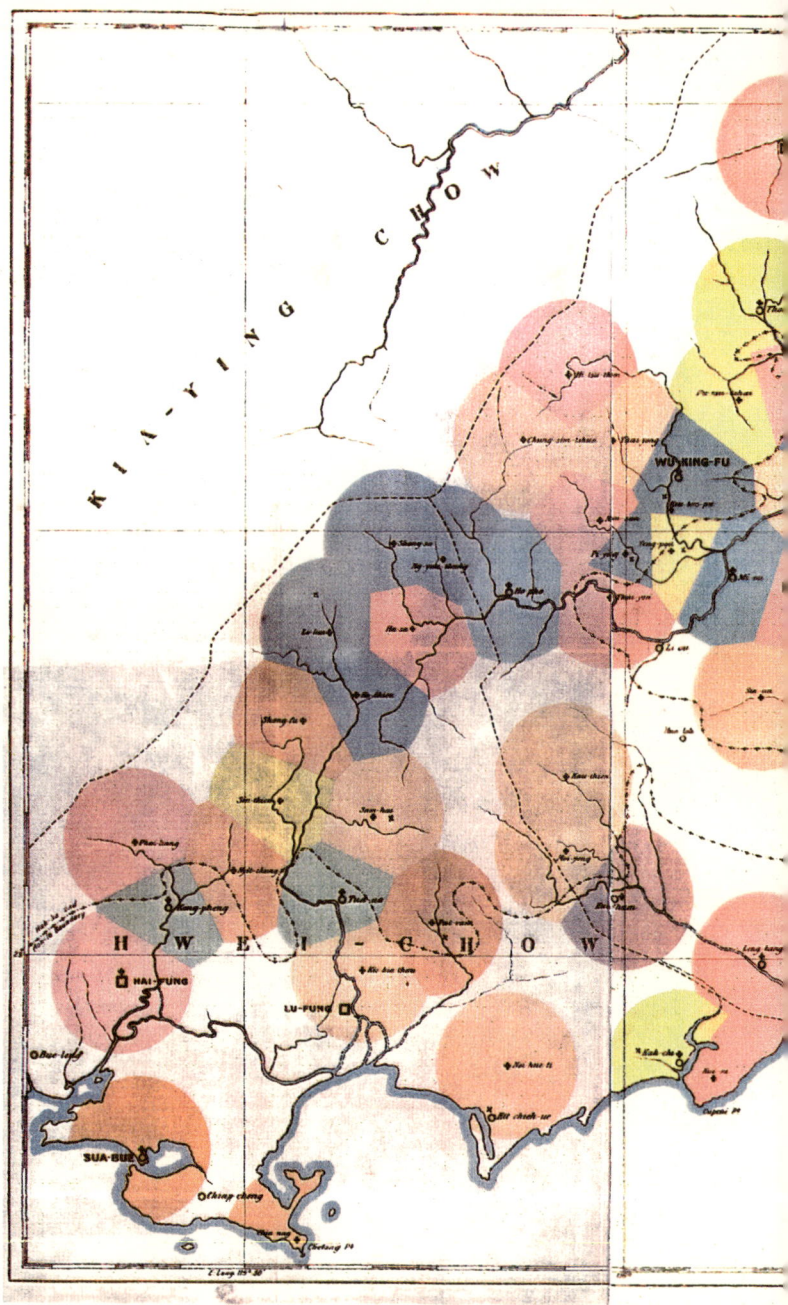

英国长老会传教士李威檩牧师绘制的传教区地图
Map of the Presbyterian Church Network in Chaoshan（1857–1900），drawn
by Rev. William Riddel

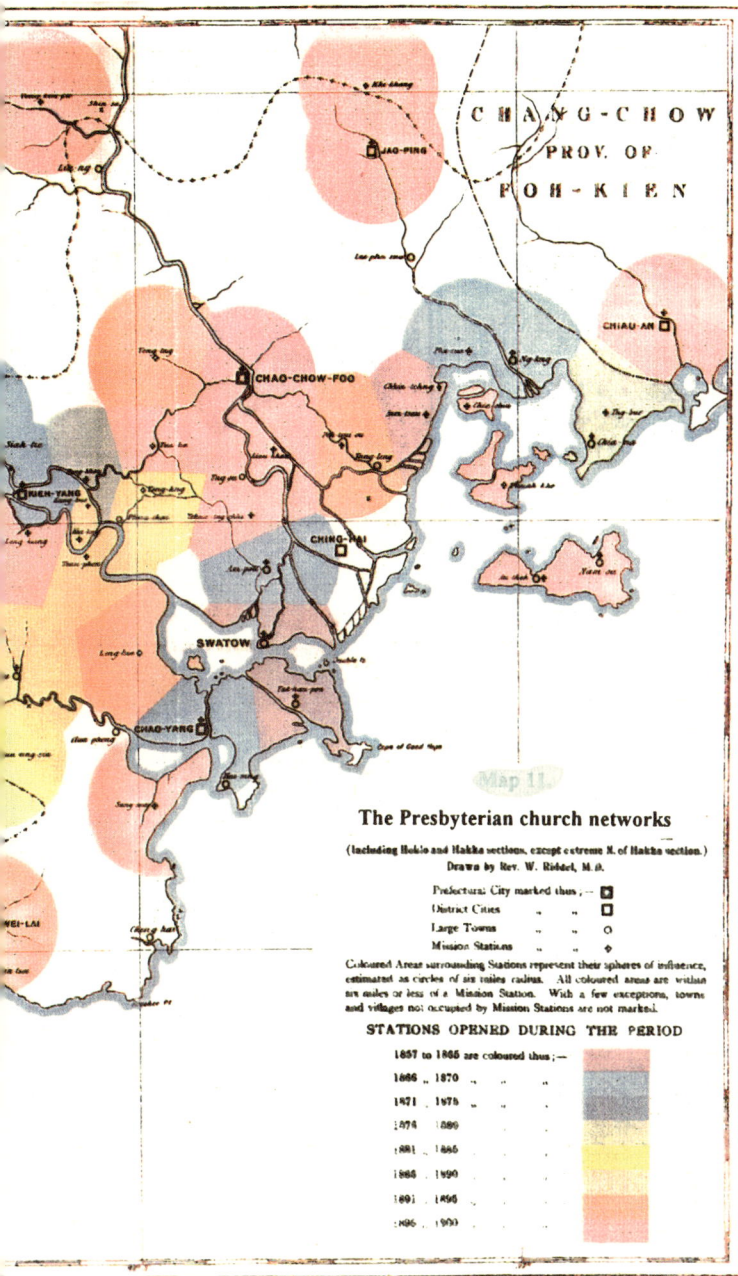

CHANG-CHOW
PROV. OF
FOH-KIEN

CHIAU-AN

CHAO-CHOW-FOO

JAO-PING

CHING-HAI

SWATOW

CHAO-YANG

Map 11.

The Presbyterian church networks

(Including Hoklo and Hakka sections, except extreme N. of Hakka section.)
Drawn by Rev. W. Riddel, M.D.

Prefectural City marked thus ; -- ▣
District Cities   "   " ◻
Large Towns   "   " ○
Mission Stations   "   " ◇

Coloured Areas surrounding Stations represent their spheres of influence, estimated as circles of six miles radius. All coloured areas are within six miles or less of a Mission Station. With a few exceptions, towns and villages not occupied by Mission Stations are not marked.

STATIONS OPENED DURING THE PERIOD

1857 to 1865 are coloured thus ; --
1866 " 1870 " " "
1871 " 1873 " " "
1874 " 1880 " " "
1881 " 1885 " " "
1886 " 1890 " " "
1891 " 1895 " " "
1896 " 1900 " " "

停泊在汕头岸边的英国长老会福音船，这是传教士到内陆河域传福音的主要交通工具

The English Presbyterian Missionaries relied on the Gospel Boat to travel to the interior

1921 年汕头港码头一隅
Landing in Shantou Harbor, 1921

大礐石村口的大闸
Gateway in Big Queshi Village

处境与视野：潮汕中外交流的光影记忆

20 世纪 20 年代初汕头市新建的马路，马路中央可见电线杆，路边两旁建有小洋楼
A newly-built street in downtown Shantou in the 1920s

汕头市道旁商店
Shops along a crowded street in downtown Shantou

汕头市火车站正门，小贩挑着货物

A scene outside the Shantou Railroad Station. Trains were off to both sides of the photograph. The man closet to the camera carried a pole on his back with two large baskets hanging from it

1921 年多位传教士乘坐手推车，头戴帽子站在车尾者为车夫
Several missionaries rode a push cart in Shantou in 1921

1923 年的汕头眼镜桥
Missionaries saw this stone bridge outside Shantou in 1923

1922年摄于汕头市郊的乡村水利灌溉系统。头戴草帽的是村丁，没戴帽子的是村童，他们脚踏抽水系统将河水排进田中

In 1922, the Baptist missionaries saw this irrigation system outside Shantou. All adults were seen wearing hats while several children were shown nearby. They all pedaled to pump water from a river to irrigate the rice field

潮阳海门湾鸟瞰图，水退时村民在沙滩上行走，下方可见今已被拆去的寨墙
A view from Haimen Bay in Chaoyang District

1929年浸信会传教士在妈屿岛度假时，摄下了这个为他们提供新鲜牛奶的牧童
When the American Baptists took a short break on Double Island in 1929, they bought fresh milk from this boy

建于潮州市韩江广济桥桥墩上的棚屋
Some old huts built on the Guangji Bridge in Chaozhou City

由舢板组成的广济桥浮桥。最吸引浸信会传教士的，除了架在水上的舢板，就是挑着担子走在桥上的老百姓

When the Baptist missionaries reached the middle section of the Guangji Bridge, they saw ordinary people walking on the pontoon and hoped to share the Gospel with them

浮桥的另一端
Another side of the Guangji Bridge in Chaozhou City

清晨潮州城内繁忙的石板老街，清洁和井然有序的街道令拍摄者赞不绝口
Ordinary people walked in both directions down a busy street in Chaozhou
City. The street was lined with shops. The boy closest to the camera walked
with a pole with two baskets attached to it. Everything looked so clean and
orderly to the missionaries

从金山回望韩江
A view of Chaozhou City from Golden Hill

潮州城内的开元寺大雄宝殿，1918年2月13日地震时屋顶受到破坏，民国初年此寺曾用于教会学校。图中两位穿马褂者是浸信会的年轻传道人，他们早年毕业于礐石学校，于20世纪20年代在准备向人布道前由传教士为其留影纪念

The famous Kaiyuan Monastery in Chaozhou City. Shortly after the 1911 Revolution, the Baptist missionaries used part of the monastery as a mission school. The roof of the monastery was damaged during an earthquake on February 13, 1918. The two young men in the photo graduated from the Baptist Boys' Academy in Shantou, and served as evangelists in the early 1920s

揭阳县城榕江边上的小楼和小船。当福音船驶近时，四名少年立刻跑到亭上供人拍摄

A view of the Rong River outside Jieyang City. Four teenagers ran to the waterfront pavilion and smiled at the missionaries. Two small boats were moored at the side of the river, and another boat was propelled by men with poles in the middle of the river

赤着身子推船的船夫
Some hardworking boatmen

每次到乡间布道，传教士都要在当地住上数天，因此福音船载满所需的衣物、食品和日用品。照片拍下了船夫、传教士的仆人和苦力在抵埠前午休

Whenever the missionaries traveled to the interior, they spent several days visiting rural congregations, bringing their own food and necessities. In this photo, boatmen and missionaries' servants took a rest during the journey

秋收时节传教士来探访，正忙于打谷的信徒乐于见到来访者
Rural Christians were pleased to see the missionaries during the autumn

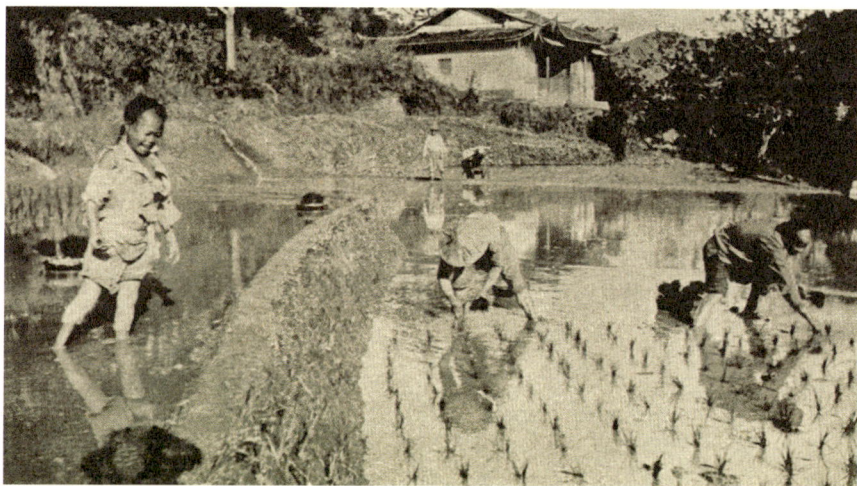

图中左方的小孩是传教士要摄拍的对象，因为他在烈日下和大人一同到田间劳作，
这令传教士大为感慨

A village boy worked in the rice field

这是个木匠，身后那张印有"上帝"字样的福音海报放在门外，让路人都可看出他的信仰

Behind this Christian carpenter was a large poster with the Chinese characters "Heavenly Lord" (Shangdi) printed on it outside the door. The carpenter was keen to share his faith with everyone

一个家庭纺织作坊。传教士在下乡探访时，会直接向妇女信徒购买制成品带回汕头转卖

These Christian women weaved fabric at home. The missionaries bought textiles from these women

赤脚的农妇在烈日下挑着两大捆的羊齿草，她皮肤黝黑，面容沧桑，见证了农民的辛劳
This woman carried a pole on her back with two large bunches of dried ferns

处境与视野：潮汕中外交流的光影记忆

盲人占卜师，他们以算命的方式为乡民趋吉避凶

This blind fortune-teller was a ritual specialist and offered advice to people about their daily problems

潮州府城外满山可见的坟墓
A hill full of tombstones outside Chaozhou City

1921 年汕头市郊的一座佛塔
A pagoda in Shantou suburb in 1921

田野上的贞节牌坊表现了乡村对传统妇德的推崇，但这为潮汕妇女带来沉重的思想包袱，传教士欲通过推广女学来改善其地位

This arch honored widows who did not remarry. Because Chaoshan women ived in a patriarchal environment, Christian missionaries developed Biblewomen training institutes and girls' schools to empower women

河婆镇所供奉的三山国王神像，此类民间神明正是传教士的对手
This shrine in Hepo market town honored the Three Mountain Kings. These deities were the missionaries' competitors to the Christian God

天后娘娘
The Empress of Heaven in a village shrine

处境与视野：潮汕中外交流的光影记忆

千手观音
The Thousand−armed Goddess

第二章　办学兴才

20 世纪初的清王朝知道，若想保住江山，改革势在必行。于是清政府在 1905 年决定废除科举考试制度，并在全国推行西方现代教育。

在这种新的政治氛围之下，全国各地包括潮汕地区在内的传教士和教会领袖，纷纷把握机会创办小学和中学，例如，浸信会在汕头对岸建立礐石中学，长老会在汕头建立华英中学。除了传福音之外，传教士的教育理想还包括：通过近代知识的传授，因应并推动中国社会的变革。这一教育理想的践行，可见于教会学校的课程设置中。学校积极推广西方的科学与技术知识，让学生能够掌握最新的技能，在剧变的商业、教育、医疗和宗教管理各专业领域中力争一席。

许多潮汕父母深知拥有现代学历与外语能力，有助于子女前途的开拓，因此乐意把子女送入教会学校读书。民间对西方教育的深切渴望，以及对教会办学的热切拥戴，一反自清末以来仇洋反教的排外情绪，显示了中国社会自义和团事件之后对现代化的迫切追求。

本章照片说明教会学校为潮汕子弟开启了一个新平台，使他们接触到新思想、新价值观、新学习法和新生活。教会学校的教育与传统教育的一个区别是，前者课程中有体育运动，特别是团体运动，包括足球、排球、篮球和田径运动。传统文人将体力劳动与社会阶层画上等号，体力劳动非儒生所为。但当体育运动成为课程的一部分，学生就必须参与。在方兴未艾的民族主义背景之下，个人体质被视为国家能力的缩影。学生把这种竞争的文化精神内在化，通过运动场上的切磋，充分表现自我以及对学校群体的支持。这种潜移默化的教学法，对培养年轻人认同现代国家公民这个新的集体身份起了一定作用。

教会学校除了作为学习知识的新空间之外，更成为孕育了一种跨越传统家庭、宗族、乡村的人际网络的场所。照片中的崇拜、毕业礼、校友会等活动，象征了一个新群体的形成，本来分散于各地各乡的潮汕青年，因为教会学校里的共同生活，成为学生、信徒、毕业生。这些共同的独特经验与回忆，以及由此所延伸的、以学校为主体的身份认同，在照片中跃然纸上。

潮汕女子教学是照片的另一个主题。中国男权当道的社会文化对妇女造成了压迫和伤害，传教士对此深表同情。传教士相信，唯有通过教育才能帮助妇女摆脱命运的桎梏，让她们得以有尊严地过上独立自主的人生。众多成功的例子包括，长老会的汕头淑德女校和汕尾嘉德女校、浸信会的汕头正光女校和河婆培光女校，这些学校初期以培训大龄女信徒阅读《圣经》为主，后来发展成教育信徒子女读书识字。晚清社会并不大注重女子教育，因此，由传教士向低下阶层推广的妇学和女学，大大提高了妇女的文化水平和个人自尊。潮汕地区不少"传道姨"在教会学校受训完毕之后，就会返回乡间传福音和建教会，从某种意义上，她们可说是当地的新一代女性。

最后，神学训练是现代教育的重要一环。浸信会礐石的天道神学院、长老会汕头贝理神学院、长老会客语地区的观丰书院，皆为有志投身传道事业的信徒提供了有系统的培训，课程包括《圣经》研究、基督教神学思想、教会管理、教会历史和宗教礼仪。这些学校栽培了一批又一批扎根本土、事奉教会、服务社会的神职人员，不但为基督教实践"自治、自养、自传"的目标提供了土壤，并且促进宗教对话，丰富了中国文化的内涵。

Chapter 2　Mission Education

In the early twentieth century, the Qing imperial government realized that China could not survive without modernizing herself. Therefore, the central government abolished the civil service examination system and introduced a Western-style education system.

In the new political climate, there was a rush among missionaries and church leaders to build modern schools such as the Presbyterian-run Anglo-Chinese College in Shantou and the Baptist-run Swatow Boys' Academy in Queshi. The planning of these Western-style schools reflected the convergence of the missionaries' vision of modern learning and the ambitions of the local Chinese elite. These schools set out to promote new ideas of science and modernization, and to equip students with the necessary knowledge to pursue careers in business, education, medicine, and church ministry.

Many Chaoshan parents fully understood the long-term benefits of an English-taught modern education and the importance of highly specialized skills in a fast-changing world for native sons. The admiration for Western-style education coincided with the growing Chinese desire for modernization in the post-Boxer era.

The following photos clearly illustrate that the advent of Western-style education opened the doors to new ideas, values, pedagogical practices, and lifestyles, thereby enlightening young people and expanding their horizons. In the mission schools, a widespread conversion to science and technology took place in dramatic fashion. The introduction of team sports like basketball, soccer, and volleyball, was a welcoming innovation to teenagers. Historically, Chinese associated any form of excessive physical exercise with poor laborers and considered it to be inappropriate for a Confucian scholar. When sports were incorporated into the modern curriculum, physical exercise became immensely popular among students. In an age of rising nationalism, being physically strong was held as an individual and collective source of pride in China. Interscholastic contests in track and field provided a valuable outlet to vent sociopolitical frustration and discontent. These features marked a significant step in China's search for modernity in the educational sphere.

The photos also indicate that troubled by the pains and sufferings of Chaoshan women in a patriarchal environment, foreign missionaries developed Biblewomen training institutes and girls' schools to raise awareness among women. The Presbyterian-run Shunde School was known for training many Biblewomen. In late imperial China, when women were not taught to read and write, Bible classes enabled them to acquire basic literacy skills and develop a sense of self-esteem and confidence. Some of these graduates returned to their home villages to found house churches, which offered them a new platform to enhance their sociocultural status.

Once Christianity had rooted itself in market towns and villages, more church-run elementary and secondary schools were founded by the local congregations in the interior. Seminaries were built by the Baptists and Presbyterians to train full-time church workers, giving them a systematic theological training. The numerous photos of campus activities, graduation ceremonies, and alumni reunions not only document the Christian students' friendship and attachment to each other but also serve as a visual symbol of their identity as part of a communitas.

1907 年美国浸信会在礐石的天道神学院，为有志投身传道事业的信徒提供系统的培训

In 1907，the Ashmore Theological Seminary was under construction. Together with the Presbyterian—run Barbour Theological College，the Ashmore Seminary provided full—time church workers with a systematic theological training

1922 年汕头礐石的浸信会传教总部
The American Baptist Mission Compound in Queshi in 1922

1922年刚竣工的浸信会礐石中学学生宿舍，全幢大楼以花岗石兴建，可容纳住宿生二百人，宿舍二楼、三楼可见入住的青年学生

This stone dormitory was built in 1922 to accommodate 200 students of the Baptist Boys' Academy

1910年英国长老会华英中学的运动会，学生通过运动场上的切磋，表现自我和对学校群体的支持。除学生之外，家长、传教士和中外商人也出席这次运动会，为学生健儿打气

This students' sports competition was held at the playground of the Presbyterian-run Anglo-Chinese College in 1910. The event was well-attended by foreign residents, missionaries, Chinese merchants, and local church members

长老会华英中学的《华英杂志》上刊登的本校全体教员照片
A group photo of teaching staff of the Anglo-Chinese College

華　　　期　二　第　年　七　圖　民　　　誌　雜

論說　三

論中國早婚之弊　　　　　　蔡紹元

夫婦爲人倫之本風化之原故首乾坤風始關雎皆以室家雍穆如鼓瑟琴爲人生之至樂雖然失之太早則兒女情長英雄氣短少年壯志常隳是以消磨過緩則曠夫怨女鬱其感情而標梅之詩作焉故古禮男三十而娶女二十而嫁循人情適中之節而爲之制意至良法至美也然中國人常欲種族繁盛之故而爽其結褵之期雖以文王猶且達之何況他人

萬民之率然十五而生武王則其早婚可知矣禮法常定於周文王猶達之何況他人

論說　四

平或謂體魂發達而故緩其配偶抑其情慾則穴隙相窺踰牆相從之弊有因是而起者矣英法患人滿之故定緩結婚之律卒之風俗淫亂比鄉衛濮上桑間而更甚此其徵也然果體魂發達而早婚之尙可言也但循是爲例蓋有軀幹幼稚而亦濫爲之矣其弊可勝言哉據醫書所紀諸名醫所經驗謂早婚者以血脈不足所生子女類多柔弱吾國人多寡小類靡不振歐洲人多強大氣宇軒昂其原因雖不一而早婚其甚者也同生天地之間而大小相反非無故而然也且中國三代以前其人種之偉大有足稱矣文王十尺

曹交九尺四寸六尺以下謂之兒今猶是人而高者尙不及兒童之數而十尺九尺者未聞爲然則謂人種薄弱於早婚無關吾未信也夫年當少壯蓬勃氣吐風雲如蒼鷹揚空猛虎嘯谷頭角崢嶸大眞爛漫如奇花初胎明月出掀天揭地之事業其所以藻繪乾坤經緯河嶽者常基於此而乃狎暱於圍房消耗其且力不但軀體不能健全而所以爲人之具亦無從而製成矣口腹累人之故每不能專心於學問亦其勢也富者而所以爲人之具亦無從而製成矣口腹累人之故每不能專心於學問亦其勢也

倘不以爲慮而中人之產雖免強支持轉眼而子女滿前將風塵奔走以室家而救饑恤寒之不暇又何能求完全於敎育哉雖其間具有卓越之天資志氣遠大然以室家而救饑恤寒之不暇

牟以子女而耗其心力者亦牛人生雖有百年而由少而壯而老可以有爲者二三十年

而已以此至少之光陰而消磨於床第妻子之間無論其無自立思想藉令有之欲求學則智識遲鈍欲營業則體力衰弱安往而能有爲耶然則嚴禁早婚於種族上事業上皆

有密切之關係操風化之柄者何其昧昧焉而不早爲之所也

THE SPIRIT OF SPORT

Our college may, with all modesty, claim to have been a pioneer in sport in Swatow. Football as a game was not played at all in Swatow by Chinese before we began it in the first term after the college was opened. The first athletic sports held in Swatow were organized by us and held upon our ground. And more recently we were, I think, the first to take up the new game of volley ball, which is now so widely played. It is difficult to realize now, in the midst of the present enthusiasm for games and athletics, that fifteen years ago it was a most difficult thing to persuade a body of students to play any games at all, and that the widespread interest in sport which is familiar to us is a growth of the few years which are covered by the short history of our own college.

The value of games and athletic competitions of all sorts is now admitted on all sides,—their value as a means of physical development. But games are something more than physical exercises; and, while it is a great benefit to have learned the methods of sport from the countries in which they have long been cultivated, it is a still more important thing that we should receive with them the spirit in which they have been cultivated. This spirit is not easy to define, but the following are at least some of the elements in it.

1. The desire to excel for the joy of excelling. There is a great pleasure for every right-minded man and boy in doing a thing well, and this applies to play as well as to work. Competition between schools is good, and to be encouraged, but a school should not require the spur of competition for the sound development of its games. The student who has the spirit of sport will wish to make himself as good a player or athlete as possible, not merely for the "name" or the prize that he hopes to win, and will wish for his school that its sports should be of the best quality, quite apart from winning matches or flags. And the player who plays slackly except when matches or contests come, has not the spirit of sport.

— 2 —

2. Appreciation of the excellence of others. The true sportsman loves to see the game played well, no matter by whom, whether by a fellow student against whom he is competing in sports, or by another school against which his is playing a match. He desires nothing but that those who play the best game should get the honours, and if that means that he loses, he accepts defeat with a cheerful and generous temper. There is no pleasure in winning unless one deserves to win because of superior strength or skill. The spirit of sport includes a hearty admiration for rivals and competitors who can beat us in a fair field.

3. Willingness to do teamwork. Players who are together in a team must learn to work, not each one for himself, but all for the team. The selfish player in any team, who only wishes to show his own skill, and wants to get the best place in order to show it, only spoils the work of the whole team; and so also does the player who will not trouble to exert himself, who will not come out to practise, or do his best when he does come out, because he thinks that he does not need to practise as much as the others; and the player who will not take instructions from his captain. A sense of duty to the team is part of the spirit of sport.

4. A hearty contempt for all that is unfair and dishonourable. This includes a strict observance of the rules of the game, but it includes more. There are players who seem to try to go as near as possible to breaking the rules without actually breaking them and coming into collision with the umpire. These are not true sportsmen. And it sometimes happens that one has a chance of getting an advantage over a competitor or an opposing team which is not forbidden by any rules, and yet is unfair; and in these cases the spirit of sport must show itself. If ever we are in doubt whether an advantage may be fairly taken or not, the surest means of testing is to ask how we should feel about it if our opponent took such an advantage of us.

All this and much more is summed up in English schools in the

— 3 —

in Swatow, let us also lead the way in showing the true spirit of sport. May it never be said of any of us or of our teams that we do not "play the game."

H. F. W.

《华英杂志》上刊登的英文文章
《运动的精神》
An article on sportsmanship published in the *Anglo–Chinese College Journal*

1915 年 11 月在汕头市举行的全市校际运动会，是日上下午都有运动竞赛，有一千多名师生参加。美国浸信会传教士耶琳夫人的日记对这次运动会有详细记载。她参观了上午的跑步和跳远赛事。照片捕捉了礐石中学男生在开幕礼上表演叠罗汉的情景，他们手持民国国旗，身穿现代体育服，充分表现了作为新时代公民的骄傲。耶琳夫人特别提到，该班男生在赛前曾受到体育老师的特训，因而赢得了多项奖牌，她为此感到十分高兴。礐石正光女校女生除了组织啦啦队之外，也参加比赛，不过她们没有赢得奖牌。另外，1930 年代中，教会学校中学生响应国民政府的新生活运动，打着旗杆参加卫生大游行

This track and field competition was held among all Chinese schools in Shantou in November 1915, with over 1,000 attendees. The program was divided into morning and afternoon sessions. Lida Scott Ashmore remarked in her diary how she watched some of the events in the morning of the competition. In the photo, students from the Boys' Academy performed a pyramid stunt as part of the opening ceremony of the competition, and won some contests. Girl students also participated in the competition. In addition, the Christian students actively participated in the public health campaign during the mid-1930s

浸信会在河婆兴建的培光女校，向下层民众推广女学，提高妇女的文化水平。楼顶的龙凤设计，甚具中国特色。在男尊女卑的环境下，地方人士对兴办女校甚为惊讶。该校致力于女子教育，最终改变了"女子无才便是德"的传统观念

In rural China, where women were not taught to read and write, Christian missionaries built modern girls' schools to empower women. The roof of this Baptist girls' school in Hepo market town was decorated in a Chinese architectural style. In Hepo, many non-Christian families sent their sons to boarding schools but were surprised to see the Baptist missionaries found a modern girls' school. The Baptist girls' school gradually changed the popular misperception of women as "no good to know much" and raised awareness among the local women

1922 年礐石男女学生参加庆祝母亲节的户外崇拜
In 1922, students gathered to celebrate Mother's Day at the Baptist Mission Compound

礐石中小学女生献唱潮语诗歌，男生在后面聆听时，一些不专心的调皮学生
不断喧哗，受到耶琳夫人和其他老师的训示
**The Baptist girls' chorus performed in front of a large crowd in Shantou. The
audience listened attentively to the singing of hymns**

1923年碣石中小学和"传道姨"穿着整齐校服，手拿证书，在毕业典礼彩排后与中外老师和传教士拍照留念

A graduation exercise for all Baptist Biblewomen and mission school girls in Queshi in 1923. The graduates wore white shirts and looked very confident. Along with them were American missionaries, Chinese teachers, and mission staff

礐石中小学在汕头其芳照相馆拍摄的教员合影
A group photo of teachers in the Baptist Girls' School

礐石妇女在美国浸信会组织下做女红，约 1911—1920 年
A group of Baptist women doing needlework in Shantou

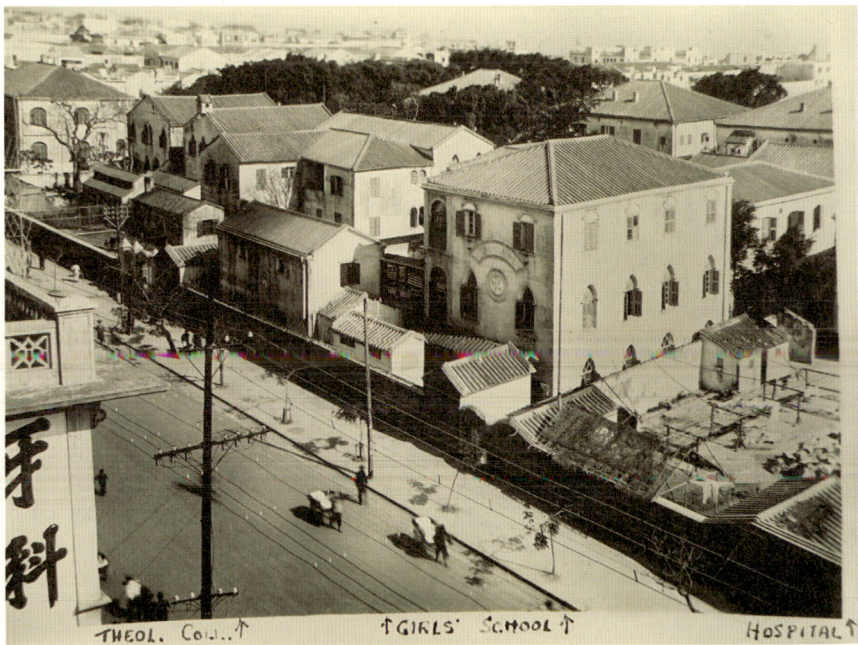

THEOL. COLL.↑   ↑GIRLS' SCHOOL↑   HOSPITAL↑

传教士在照片下方清楚记录了昔日汕头长老会的贝理神学院、淑德女校（注意校舍墙上的竹叶装饰）和福音医院的所在位置

The Presbyterian Mission Headquarters in Shantou. The photo identified the Barbour Theological College, the Shunde Girls' School, and the Gospel Hospital

处境与视野：潮汕中外交流的光影记忆

长老会传教总部内淑德女校的另一面，前方是供学生锻炼的操场
The Shunde Girls' School，inside the Presbyterian Mission Compound

淑德女校的师生围坐一圈在学习讨论
A Bible study among Presbyterian women students

长老会客语地区的女校，一位女生站在门口
The Presbyterian Girls' School in Wujingfu

五经富女校开学
Opening of the Girls' School in Wujingfu

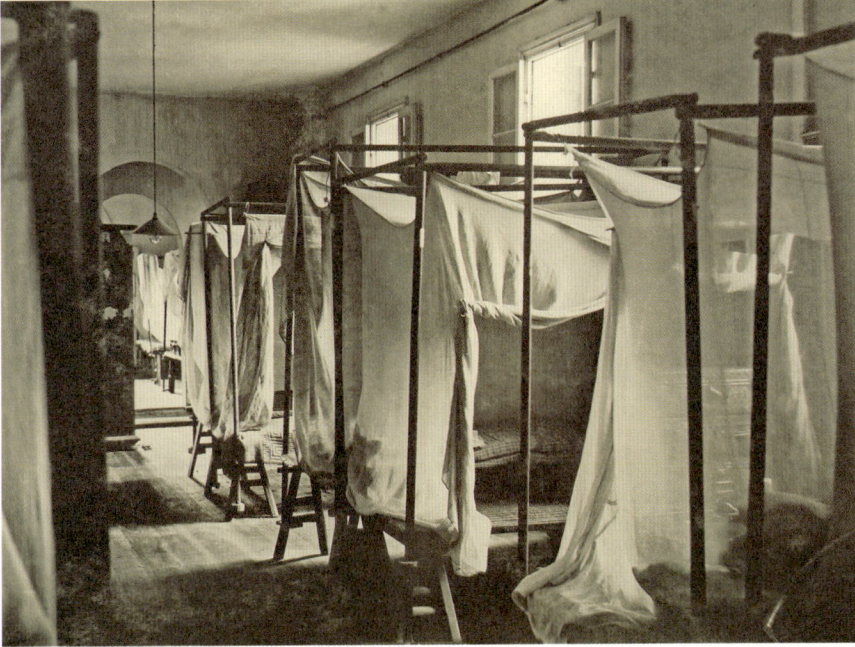

长老会淑德女校学生宿舍，每个房间可容纳八至十名女生。她们一人一床，每张床皆有独立的蚊帐，这种相对注重个人隐私的校园集体生活有别于农村的乡土文化
The Presbyterian Mission furnished sleeping quarters for Biblewomen. Eight to ten women were packed into this room with their own beds

四名长老会女子学校的亲密姐妹与她们的老师（中间站立者）合影
These four Presbyterian girls were close friends. They took this photo with their teacher (in the middle) before graduation

这四名长老会"传道姨"在 1873 年入读淑德女校，成为首届毕业生。六十年后她们返校团聚时拍下这张照片。她们手持《圣经》，没有缠足，是早期识字并且行动自由的中国女传道人

These four elderly women were among the first group of Presbyterian students to attend the Shunde Girls' School in 1873. They had a reunion in Shantou in 1934. They did not have bound feet and were very proud to carry Bibles

1933年7月1日，旅居上海的汕头淑德校友带着她们的子女与昔日传教士合照
On July 1, 1933, the alumni of the Shunde Girls' School in Shanghai had a reunion and brought their children to the event

1960 年在香港尖沙咀潮人生命堂，淑德校友与昔日的传教士恩师合照
The Shunde alumni attended a church service with their former teacher in Hong Kong in 1960

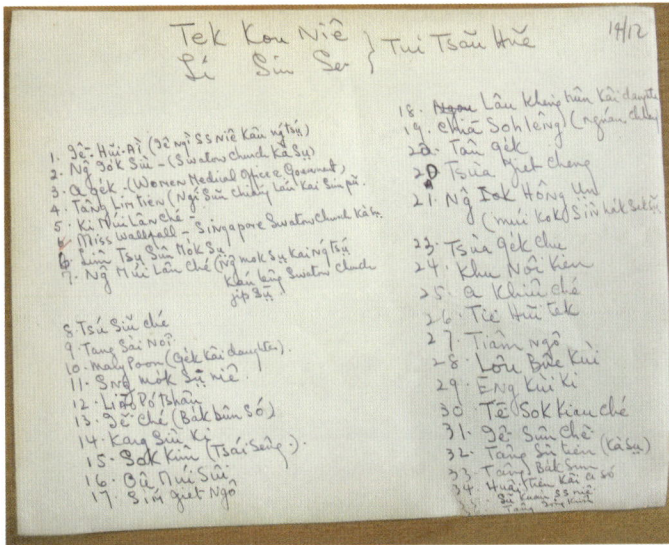

照片背面记录了 1960 年香港淑德校友们的罗马拼音潮语名字
The names of the Hong Kong Shunde alumni were written in Romanized Chaozhou dialect

马来亚淑德校友团聚，年老者是早年移居当地的汕头女信徒
A reunion among the Shunde alumni in Malaya

背面有合影者姓名，这些马来亚淑德校友大多来自潮语和客语地区的资深长老会家庭
Names of the alumni were at the back of the photograph. Many of these Shunde alumni came from the oldest Presbyterian families in the Chaozhou– and Hakka–speaking areas

她们是长老会女子学校的毕业生，在
1949 年前离开汕头前往香港定居。
1960 年她们拍下这张合照给董玛莉
校长留念
These seven alumni of the Presbyterian
Girls' School had a reunion in Hong
Kong in 1960. They left Shantou for
Hong Kong before 1949

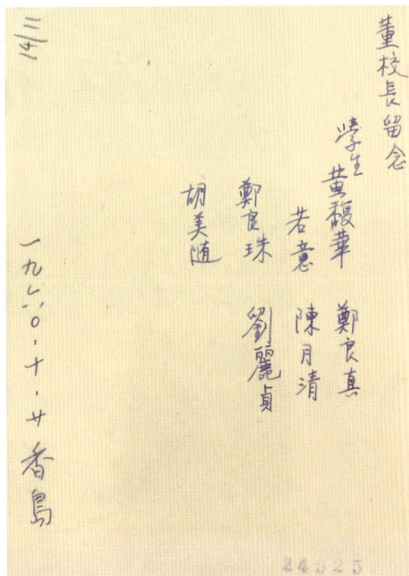

照片背面有七名女校友的名字
The names of seven alumni in Hong Kong

长老会客语地区的观丰书院开幕当天
The opening of the Presbyterian Seminary in the Hakka area

今日的观丰书院
The former Presbyterian Seminary in the Hakka area as shown today

1924年汕尾嘉德女校成立典礼，此校为当地信徒女孩提供全面的西式教育
The opening of the Shanwei Presbyterian Girls' School in 1924, providing a comprehensive Western-style education to the local Christian girl

1934 年 第二届嘉德女校毕业生（后排站立者）与青年女教员
The second group of graduates from the Shanwei Presbyterian Girls' School in 1934. The six
graduates stood confidently holding their certificates，with four young teachers sitting in front

　处境与视野：潮汕中外交流的光影记忆

汕尾嘉德女校大合影

A group photo of all members of the Shanwei Presbyterian Girls' School

黎节姑娘（前排左起第六位）在 20 世纪三四十年代在汕头传教，1951 年后前往马来亚传教直至退休。此照片是她在 1948 年与部分长老会女校校友的合影
Agnes Richards (seated, sixth from the left) was a missionary in Shantou from 1932–1941, and 1947–March 1951, and after that in Malaya until 1967. Pictured here were alumni of the Presbyterian Girls' School. Agnes Richards was seated sixth from the left

1949 年 5 月 25 日汕尾作嘉中学（作德男校与嘉德女校并校）复校后首次校庆合影。部分学生穿着童子军制服

On May 25, 1949, the Shanwei Presbyterian Secondary School gathered to celebrate its reopening after World War Ⅱ

汕尾作嘉中学附属小学 1949 年 6 月 22 日第一届，也是唯一的一届毕业生合影留念
The Shanwei Presbyterian Primary School held its first and only graduation ceremony in June 1949

　处境与视野：潮汕中外交流的光影记忆

1950年2月23日，汕尾教会欢送传教士回国时合影留念

The Presbyterian educational missionaries left Shanwei for England after many years of service on February 23, 1950

第三章　施医赠药

西方医学的传入以至植根于潮汕社会，是一个循序渐进的过程；近代医疗和护理教育的制度化，则是潮汕中西文化交流史上的重要一页。另外，施医赠药与福音传播密不可分，医疗传教的最大目的在于令病人相信，身体康复与皈依上帝是联系在一起的。传教士总是强调西方医药的先进，病人也认为信教有一定的疗效。这种把治病用作吸引信徒的传教策略，在亚非拉地区非常普遍。

在长老会创办的汕头福音医院中，传教士和传道人每天早晚都向病人布道。传教士及其同工还会给病人进行单独教导，鼓励他们摒弃烧香拜神的行为，他们试图用西方医学打开中国人接受福音之路。

每逢周二和周五，医院会进行门诊服务，急症者则可随时求医。当病人抵达医院挂号登记、等待治疗时，除拿到筹号之外，他们还会收到福音单张。传道人向患者进行布道和安慰时，特别注重他们所受到的肉体痛苦。他们通过简单的福音单张和个人面谈，深入浅出地向患者讲解基督教救赎与盼望的信息。对于那些愿意接受基督教教义的病人，传道人员会教导他们背诵十诫、主祷文，并教唱潮语诗歌赞美上帝。

如果病人不识字，传教士就选择一些简单的《圣经》篇章让他们默记。传教士希望教导病人以《圣经》作为检视人生价值观的最高标准。传教士相信，公开诵读《圣经》经文可以洗涤病人日积月累的传统宗教信仰，同时在他们的记忆里播下基督信仰的种子：皈依上帝是让身体得到康复、心灵得到救赎的唯一方法，而这种宗教不只是拜祭神明，而是肇基于有系统地认识教理、实践正确的礼仪和过一种有道德的人生。

1874 年汕头福音医院的 30 名病人中，有 5 人受洗。当病人离开医院时，传教士玛坚绣鼓励他们回家后到家乡附近的教会聚会。其中有些皈依者甚至开始在自己的村庄建立教堂，揭阳西浦村的蔡亚雷就是一个例子。他于 19 世纪 70 年代初在福音医院获得医治，回乡后就建立了一个教堂，并积极向族人传播基督教。

1884 年潮州地区的 23 个教堂中，有七八个教堂是由汕头福音医院康复的病人建立的，包括潮阳西部的贵屿、仙门城和流沙三个教堂。此外，还有康复者在医院接触福音后改变信仰，饶平县城教堂就是其中一例。该堂原是一个佛教斋堂，1888 年堂主在汕头福音医院皈依了基督教，之后他就将自己的斋堂改建成一个长老会的教堂。

作为非牟利的专业医疗机构，汕头福音医院为潮汕地区提供了可信、有效、高质素和以人为本的现代医护服务。本章照片摄于清末和第二次世界大战后，拍摄对象是渐渐复原的福音医院，从中可见随着基督教而来的近代医疗知识、科技以及卫生意识的普及化。

镜头清晰地捕捉了福音医院内医护人员、医学教授、前线员工的精神面貌。他们一身洁白的制服，自信满满地把最新、最好的治疗带给劳苦大众。特别是其中的女性医护人员，不管患者是男是女，她们都奋战在第一线，在病房、手术室和药房里恪尽职守，与男同事并肩共事。这显示了她们通过专业技能，在男尊女卑的文化环境之下，成功地营造了一个践行理想与使命的自主空间。

此外，镜头焦点下的医护人员并不是高高在上的服务施予者，病人也并非卑下无助的乞求者。相中人的表情告诉我们，治疗是基于双方的相互信任和跨越社会地位的关爱，而这正是基督教医疗事业在当地最重要的历史遗产。

Chapter 3   Western Medicine

The spread of Western biomedicine and the institutionalization of medical and nursing education constituted one of the most important chapters in the history of Sino–Western cultural encounters in Chaoshan. Medical ministry and evangelization were interdependent from the beginning of the Christian missionary movement. The strategy of outdoor preaching could be very effective when it was combined with the provision of medical services.

In the Presbyterian–run Shantou Gospel Hospital, foreign missionaries and Chinese evangelists held daily morning and evening services for patients, together with religious classes for women and children. They instructed patients to denounce traditional religious practices, revealing the missionaries' attempt to use Western biomedical skills to open the way for evangelization.

What the missionaries considered to be legitimate religion was not an icon but a corpus of textually codified doctrine. The Word occupied a preeminent position because the spread of Christianity was rooted in verbal and textual rhetoric. The Christian rituals and practices possessed meaning only in the light of doctrines and other textual materials.

When patients came to the hospitals, they received a scriptural text with their call number from a colporteur. Those patients willing to hear the gospel were taught to read the Ten Commandments, the Lord's Prayer, a few biblical passages, and to sing hymns in the Chaozhou dialect.

Because many patients were illiterate, some basic biblical passages were selected for them to memorize. The missionaries believed that they could employ public reading and memorization to purge the ingrained popular religious practices from the minds of the patients and to embed biblical messages in their memories. Memorizing the Ten Commandments, hymns, and biblical passages conveyed the idea that absolute obedience to God was a key to physical recovery and spiritual salvation.

In 1874, William K. Mackenzie reported that five of the thirty baptized church members had converted in the mission hospital. The missionaries encouraged the hospital converts to join the local Presbyterian churches near their home villages. Some of the converts even acted on their own initiative to found churches in their home villages. Cai Yalei, a native of Xibu village in Jieyang district, after his medical treatment in the early 1870s at the Shantou Gospel Hospital, returned home to set up a mission station and spread the Christian message to his kinsmen.

By 1884, seven or eight out of twenty–three Presbyterian chapels were built by former hospital patients, including congregations in Guiyu, Xianmencheng and Liusha in western Chaoyang district. Another example that illustrates the importance of the medical ministry was the opening of a chapel in the district city of Raoping. The chapel was originally a Buddhist vegetarian hall. In 1888, the wealthy owner of the vegetarian hall received medical treatment in the Shantou Gospel Hospital and converted. After he returned home, he turned the hall into a Presbyterian chapel.

The medical missionaries set out to connect healing and Christianity in the minds of patients. Since the missionaries often emphasized the superiority of Western medicine, the patients tended to perceive the new religion as a remedy against illness. This popular tendency to try out Christianity as a medical treatment was common in other mission fields in Asia, Africa, and Latin America.

Taken in the late 1940s, the following photos of the Shantou Gospel Hospital display a remarkable popularization of new medical knowledge, practices, norms and habits associated with the arrival of Christianity. The portable camera deliberately captured images of competent Chinese medical practitioners, nurses, instructors, and administrative staff, wearing professional uniforms and posed in a confident manner.

The professionally trained Chinese medical pratitioners and nurses served as cultural mediators between English medical missionaries and local patients. In particular, female doctors and nurses in Chaoshan carved out a separate space to exercise their own professional and moral leadership within the gender–segregated hospital, and to assert their agency in China's patriarchal society.

Furthermore, the visual focus here is not necessarily on well–trained medical staff as service–providers and poor patients as receipents, but rather on the reputation of the Gospel Hospital for its reliable and high–quality care, and a burning desire to heal the sick and serve the poor. This is the most important legacy of the Christian medical ministry in Chaoshan.

潮汕地区最初的宗教宣传广告，长老会周日聚会时间表，同时列出长老会教堂位置、医院服务。左下方文字："其施济医馆，设在汕头汛地前，凡治病日期定于拜二、拜五。若是急症，不论时日皆可得医。其间不特治病，亦得听真理焉。"

This 1880 Christian wall calendar listed the dates of Sunday service, the location of Presbyterian chapels in Chaoshan, and the medical services for outpatients at the Gospel Hospital every Tuesday and Friday

1949 年汕头福音医院中外医护人员的合影，这所医院是 19 世纪以来中英合作的医疗机构和医护人员培训中心

Chinese and English medical staff at the entrance of the Gospel Hospital in Shantou in early 1949. The photo revealed the Sino–British partnership in providing medical services to the Chaoshan region

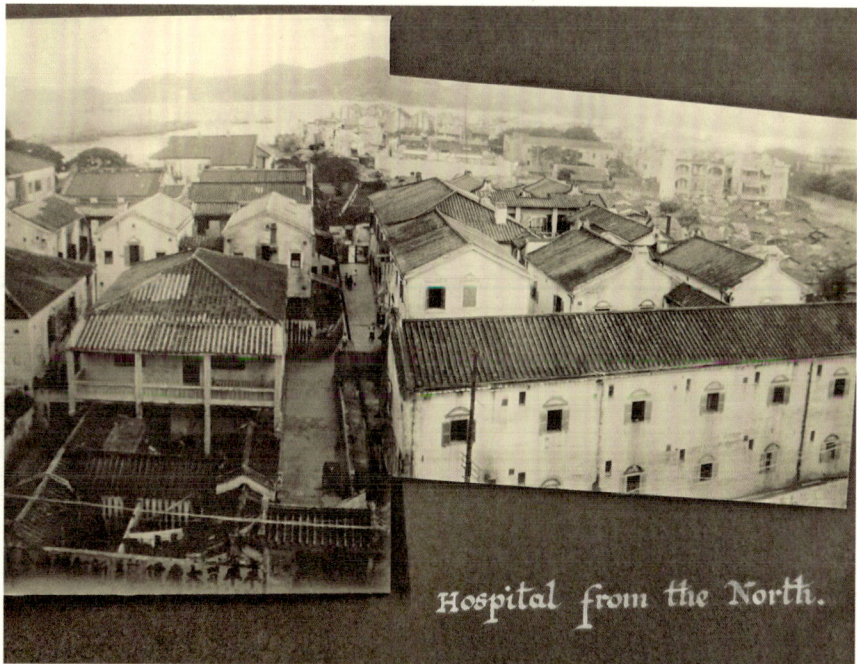

从汕头市中心向南瞭望，照片前方大楼皆为福音医院建筑，远处可见汕头港和对岸礐石一带
The Gospel Hospital viewed from the north. Shantou harbor and Queshi were in the background

汕头福音医院的庭院空地
The Gospel Hospital courtyard

汕头福音医院侧影
Another view of the Gospel Hospital

福音医院与淑德女校毗邻而立，英国护士长在浇花，女学生在散步
The Gospel Hospital was located next to the Shunde Girls' School, inside the Presbyterian Mission Compound. Students took a walk in the garden during a break

医院每逢周二和周五提供门诊服务，病人要在大清早就到医院门外等候，其中不少人来自边远农村地区

Over twenty patients queued outside the Gospel Hospital. Some patients walked over long distance and difficult terrain to get medical treatment in Shantou

揭阳西浦村的蔡亚雷于19世纪70年代初在福音医院获医治，回乡后建立教堂。蔡亚雷曾经就像这些在福音医院候诊的病人一样

An old photo showed patients waiting inside the courtyard of the Gospel Hospital in the late nineteenth century. Some of them, like Cai Yalei, a native of Xibu village in Jieyang district, converted and returned home to set up mission stations

病人在挂号处办理登记手续，登记人员在此把筹号和福音单张交给病人
Patients waiting to receive their call number in the reception area

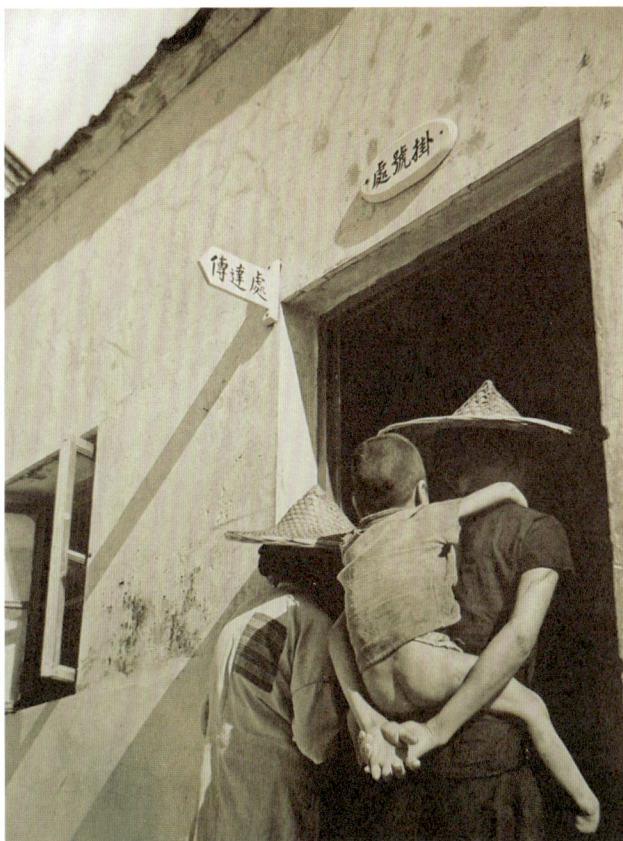

贫苦大众来福音医院求医
A woman with a child patient on her back came for medical treatment

有脚患的老人

An elderly patient with foot injuries

求医的赤足妇人
A barefoot woman came to the hospital

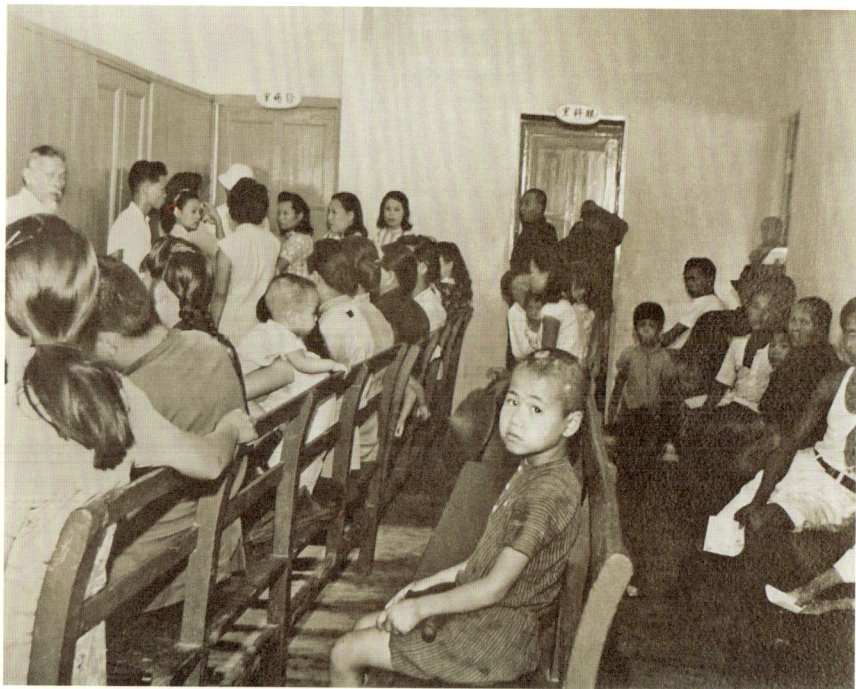

求医者不少是幼童和妇女

Over twenty patients sat in the crowded waiting area, including many children and women

一位退休牧师和两位"传道姨"在候诊室向病人传福音，并唱圣诗《靠近十字架》
A retired Presbyterian pastor and two Biblewomen spoke to outpatients in the waiting area. They told biblical stories and sang hymns in the Chaozhou dialect, such as "Jesus, Keep Me Near the Cross"

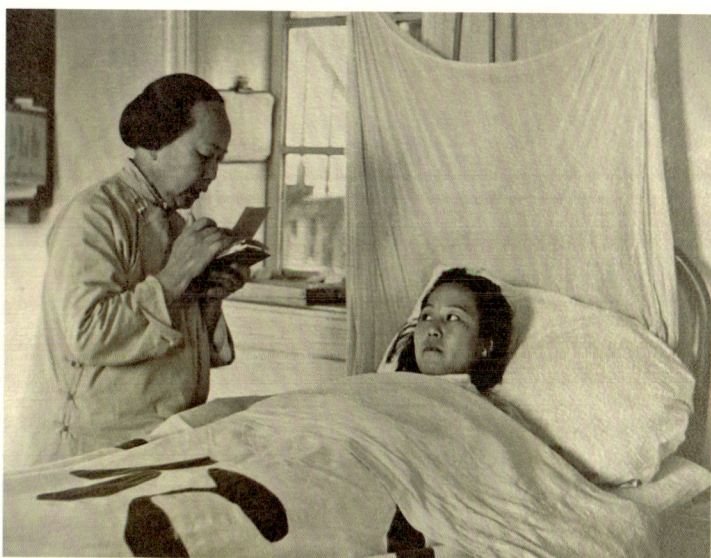

"传道姨"向女病人分享福音
A Biblewoman speaking to a female patient

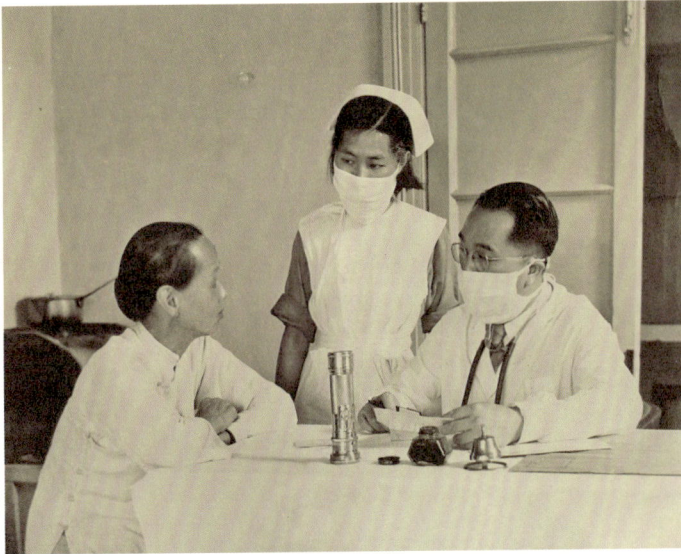

医生向女病人问症，医护都戴有口罩，可能当时是传染病旺季
A doctor treated a female patient. Doctors and nurses wore masks during an
epidemic

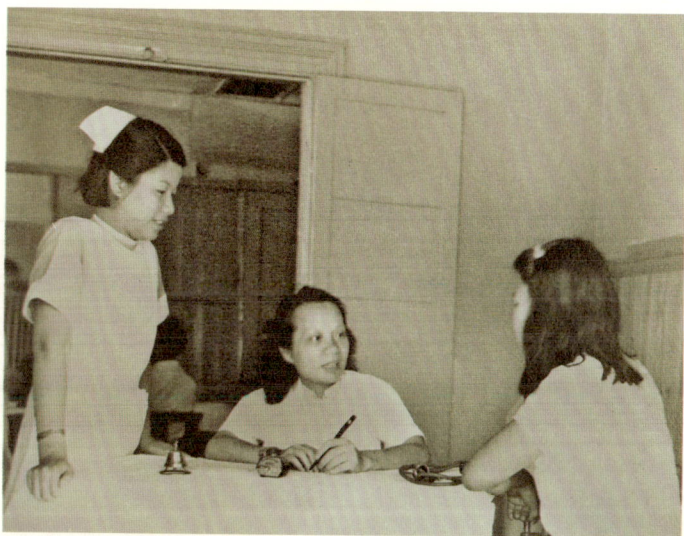

正在诊断的女医生
A female doctor giving a patient consultation

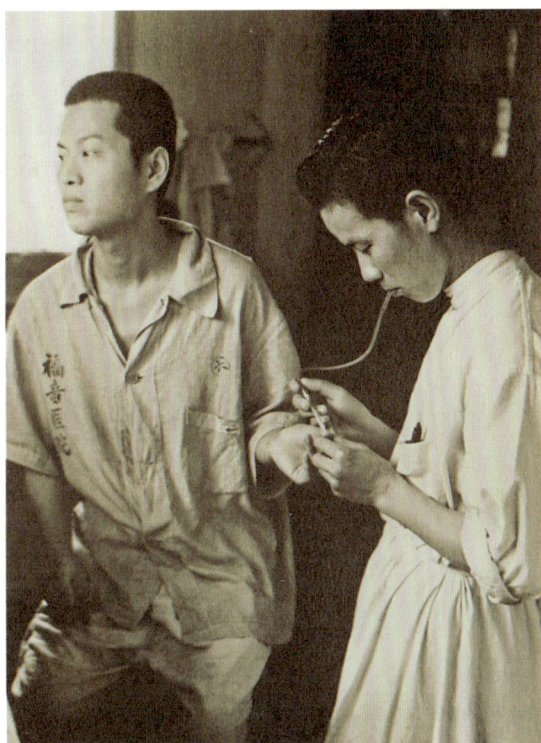

病人接受抽血
A nurse performed a blood test

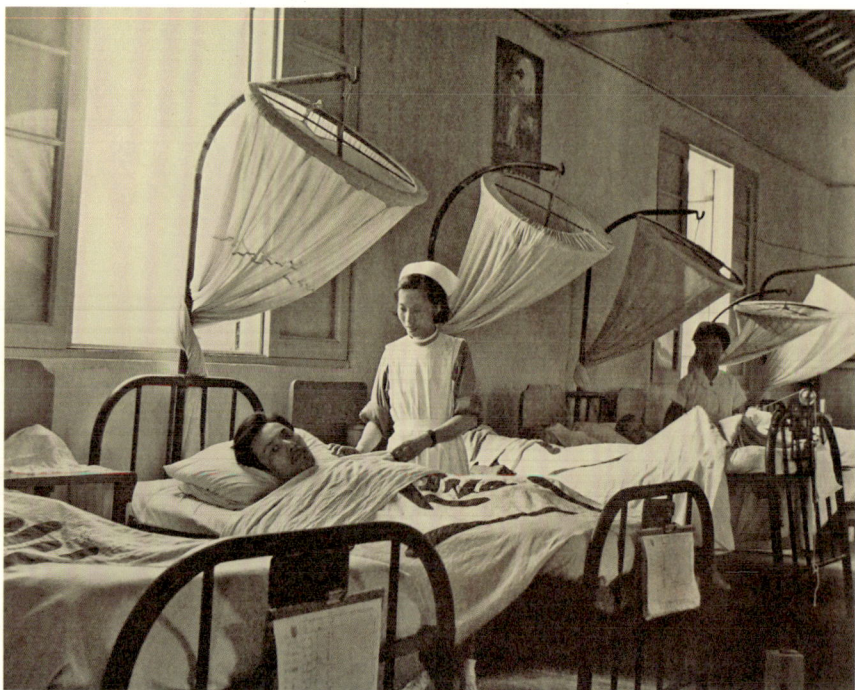

病房的设计充满基督教氛围，信、望、爱是基督教的精神信仰，被单有"信"字，墙上挂有耶稣画像

A male ward inside the Gospel Hospital. The male patient was covered with a blanket with the character "Faith" written on it, and there was a drawing of Jesus on the wall

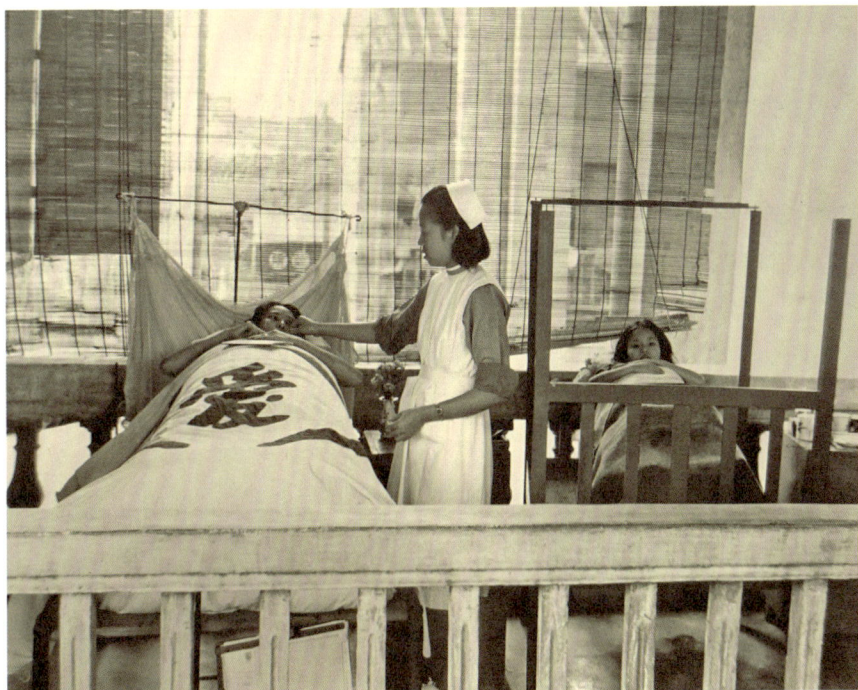

女病房一角印有"爱"字的被单

A female ward. The female patient on the left was covered with a
blanket with the character "Love" written on it

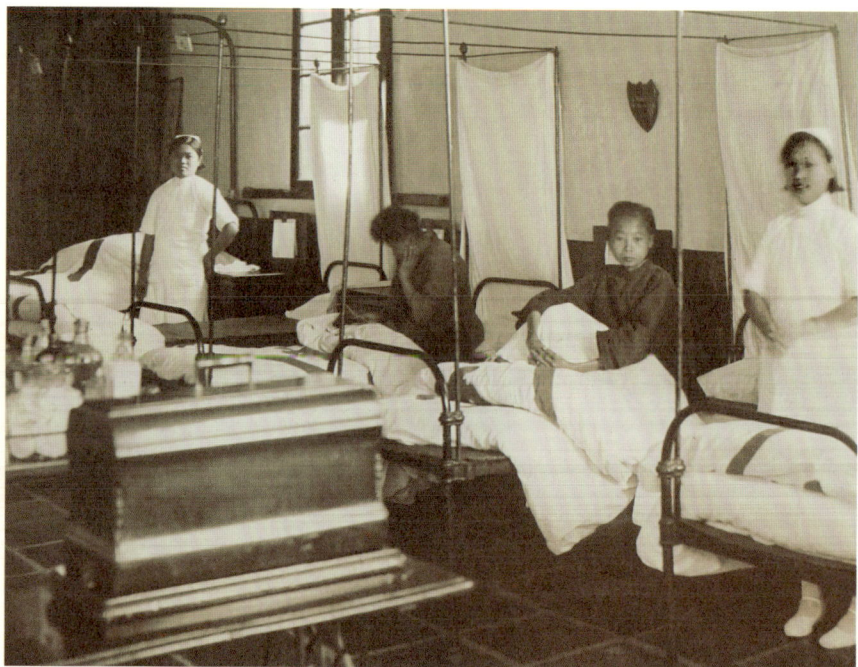

女病房
A female ward

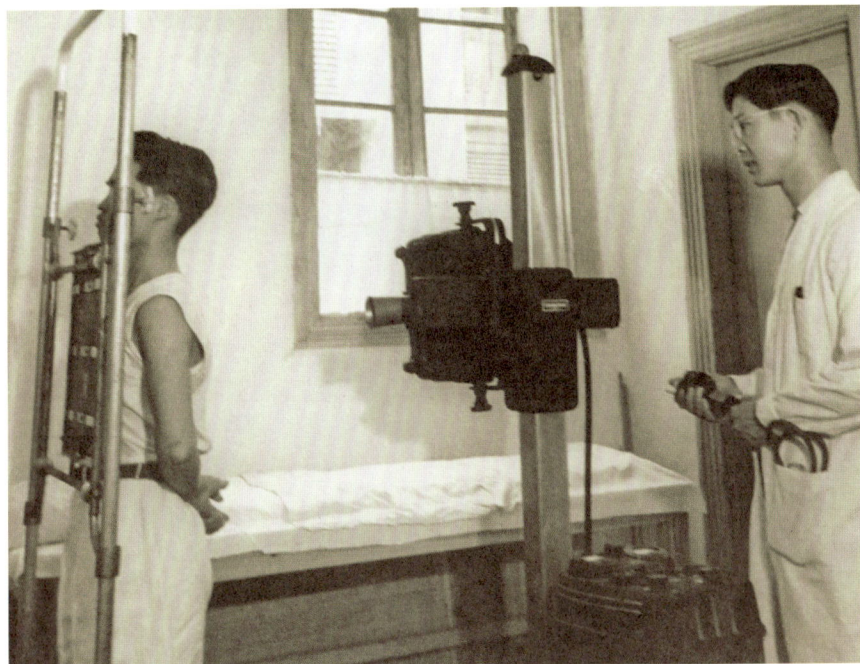

汕头福音医院的 X 射线装置
X-ray facilities inside the Gospel Hospital

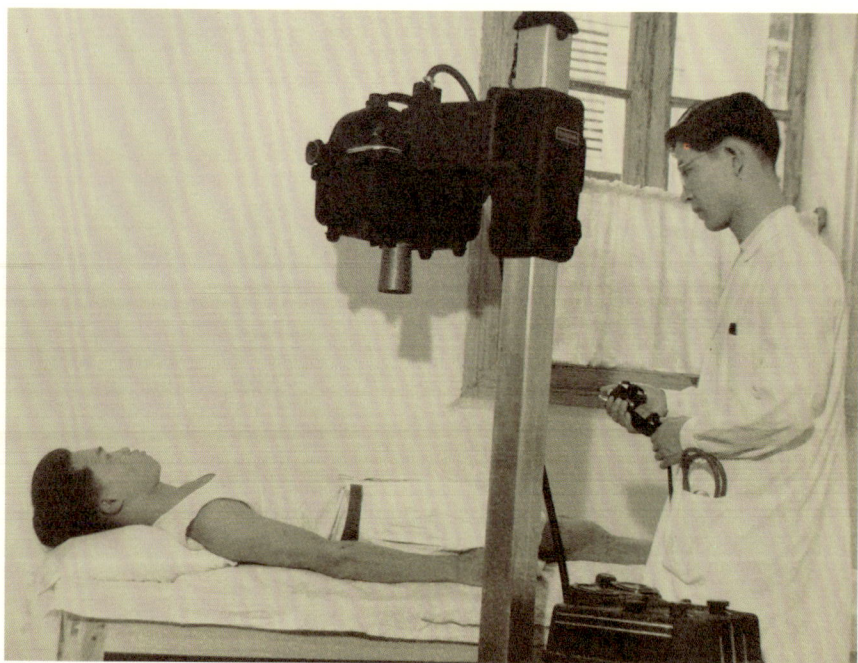

病人接受 X 射线检查

A patient took an X-ray test

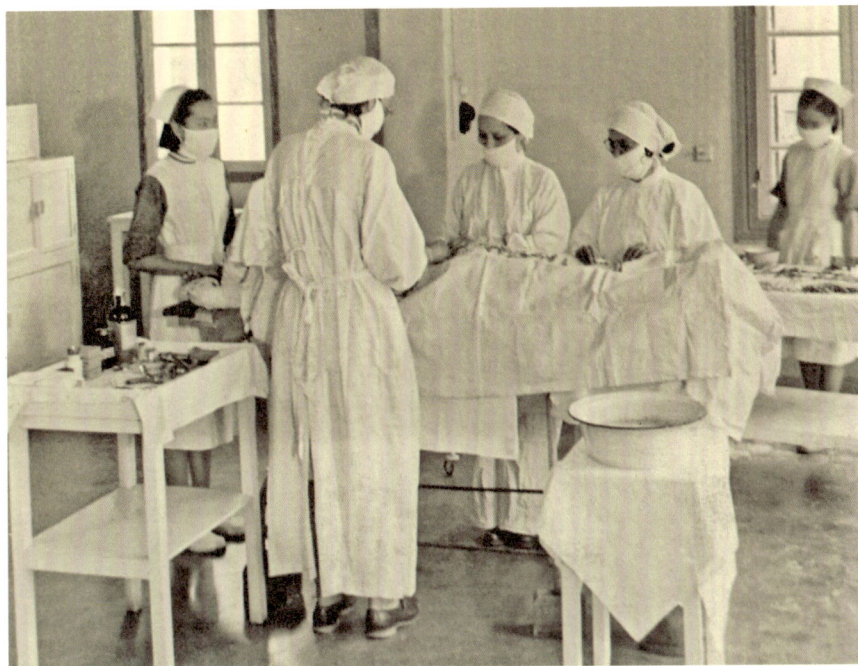

手术进行中
A surgery underway

药房

The medicine storage

器具房
Storage

经常打扫，保持卫生

A janitor who kept the place tidy and clean

清洗干净后的病床用品，在烈日下晒干消毒
Drying bedsheets in the courtyard

三人在碾米，把稻谷碾过后，米和谷壳（潮汕人称"谷壳"为"粗糠"）被分开，
粗糠落在地下，米流进箩筐中

The kitchen staff grinded rice

准备膳食
The kitchen staff prepared meals

为病人做饭
The kitchen staff prepared meals for patients

病人用膳
A male ward during lunchtime

医院员工准备用膳

The hospital staff cooked meals for themselves

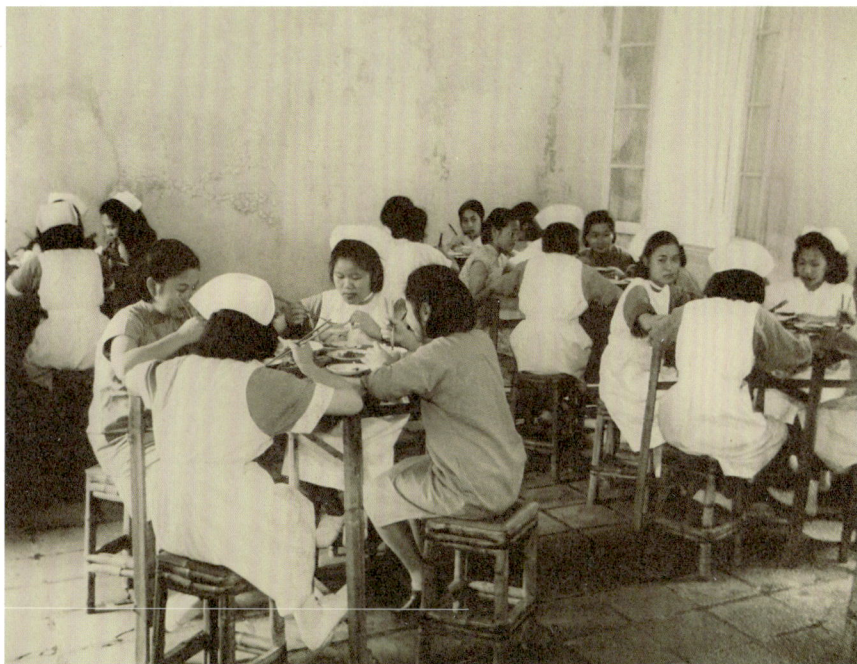

学护（没有帽子）与护士实习生一同用膳
Nursing students (without hats) and interns had lunch in the hospital canteen

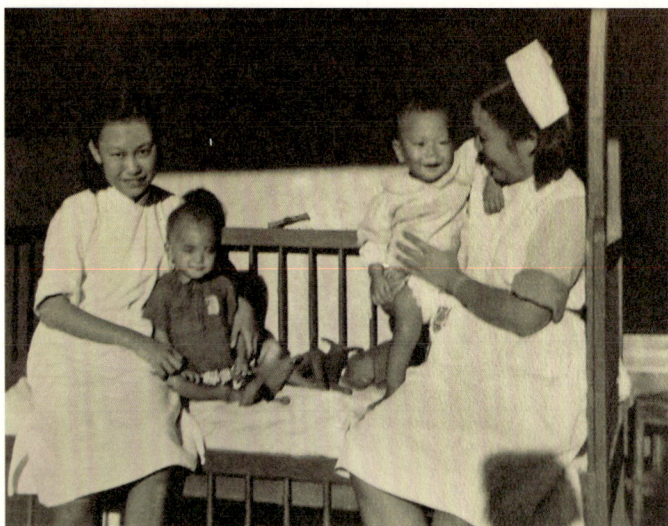

两名病童在悉心照料下康复
Two babies recovering from illnesses in the children's ward

Two of the Nurses, with 2 of the babies [9/53] the Children's ward — on the R. a 3rd year nurse with a baby whose parents died in Hospital (left behind by Nationalist Army) — if the relatives in the North cannot send for him from the North Anhui this Nurse's family wants to adopt him. On the L. a probationer nurse who is not yet 'capped' (ie has not finished her 4 months probation) with a baby who when she came in was a mere bag of skin + bones + so weak she could not lift her head — now she is like the Cheshire cat — one big grin of joy — all day long!

传教士在照片背面仔细记录了两名病童的经历。右方小童是安徽人，其父亲为国民党退役士兵，与妻子在福音医院中去世，成为孤儿的小童无亲人认领。手抱他的护士准备将他领养。左边护士实习生手抱的女孩，入院时身体虚弱，严重营养不良，头、手、脚都不能移动，经抢救后慢慢康复
The medical history of the babies

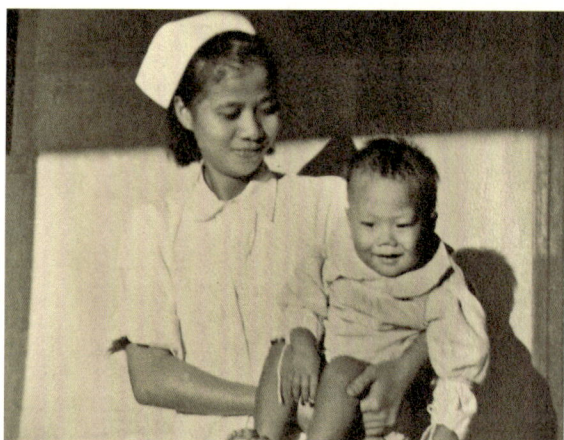

安徽小童与另一名护士合影
The baby from Anhui Province and other nurse

另一位住院病童
A child with head injuries

遗弃在福音医院外被收容的小孩。抱着他们的保姆来自底层的教会家庭，因为种种原因落难汕头，于是寄居在医院中，被雇用照顾这些孤儿

Nurses and nannies fed the orphans inside the hospital

护士实习生毕业典礼

A graduation ceremony for nursing students

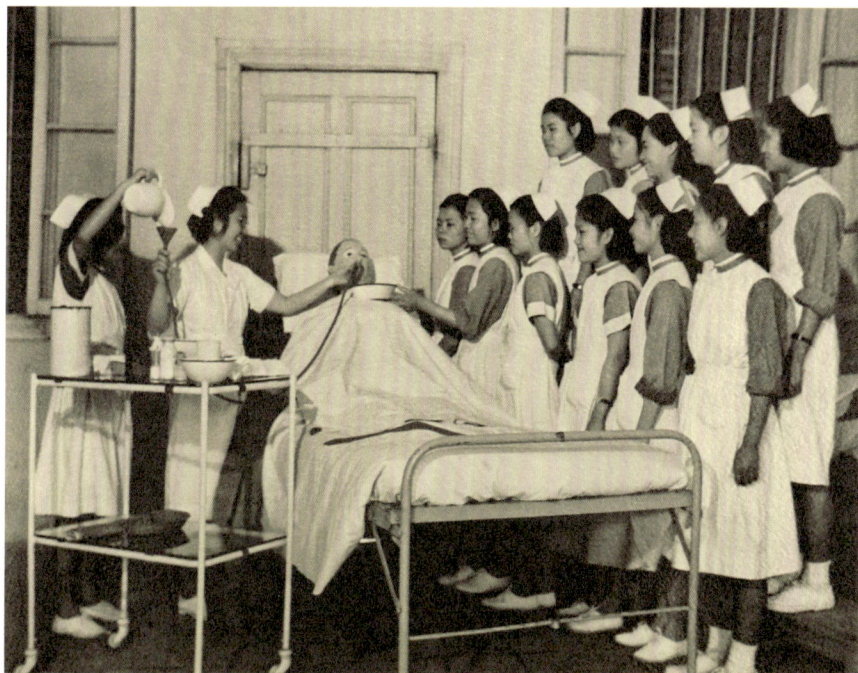

护士实习生学习喂食
A demonstration of feeding a patient

护士学生上课，女生坐在前排，男生坐在后排
Nursing students attended a lecture, girls in front while boys at back

护士学生与中学女生打篮球

Nursing students and mission school girls enjoyed a basketball game

护士实习生合影
A group photo of nursing interns

医护传教士（中间站立者）与院内同工
A group photo of doctors and staff

院内女同工

A group photo of female hospital workers

院内男杂役

A group photo of male hospital laborers

美国浸信会在远离汕头的河婆镇建立了大同医院，以服务内陆地区
The American Baptist Hospital in Hepo market town

第四章 赈灾施善

一段虹霓出海隅，八风如战雨倾衢。

楼头绿树连根拔，陌上青秧贴水枯。

正拟望秋差有庚，那思卒岁更无襦。

推窗一望天初霁，早有排年说晚租。

——李质

　　明代诗人李质的这首诗，讲述了台风对潮汕社会与经济所造成的灾害。自古以来潮汕一直受到台风、地震和水患的困扰。天灾造成了极为严重的人命与财产损失，以致潮汕当地士绅与官员必须联手赈灾才能纾解民困。然而随着清朝没落，民国政府又未能稳住新政权，一旦发生天灾就不得不由民间组织来主持赈济的工作。美国浸信会和英国长老会对赈灾的投入尤其明显。

　　本章照片围绕着三场天灾——1911 年 9 月的水灾、1918 年 2 月 13 日的地震、1922 年 8 月 2 日的风灾——展开，显示了灾难的严重性和教会在进行赈灾时所面对的困难。

1911 年 9 月的水灾

　　就在辛亥革命爆发前的一个月，1911 年 9 月 8 日和 9 日的连场暴雨把韩江下游城镇一概淹没。9 月 12 日，潮汕铁路因为被大水淹没而完全瘫疾，两个城市的交通中断。韩江水势汹汹，农田和村落都被恶水吃尽。堤坝保不住泛滥的韩江下游流域，下游的百姓纷纷跑到高地避难。

美国浸信会派遣先头部队到灾场进行实地考察，发现几千人在堤道上扎营等候水退。某些水位已经下降的地区，灾民已经回到残破不堪的坏房子进行抢修；可是低洼地带却仍然受到恶水围困，那里的灾民正在等待救济。

于是英美传教士在 9 月 11 日成立了一个委员会。这个潮州水灾救助委员会是一个跨阶层、跨种族的组织，由英国长老会牧师汲约翰任主席，其他成员包括有名望的商人，来自英、美、德三国的领事官员，还有汕头海关专员。中外教会在官方以外联手实施救援行动，并通过地方信徒把救灾物品送到灾民手中。

1918 年 2 月 13 日的地震

除了季节性水灾之外，潮汕沿岸地区还广泛受到南澎列岛及其邻近水域的地震影响。最严重的一次发生在 1918 年 2 月 13 日下午 2 时 7 分。

浸信会传教士何范克在渡过汕头港口时目击地震导致"汕头和礐石的上空灰烟四起"。因坐落在布满岩石的礐石斜坡上，美国浸信会的传教总部在地震期间只受到轻微损毁，可是汕头市和南澳岛却伤亡惨重，耶琳夫人这样记述道：

> 汕头市街道狭窄，房子倒下时人们都走避不及，许多人被埋在瓦砾之中。几天前存心善堂才捐出了 140 具棺木……南澳岛上的主要市集都被夷为平地，死亡人数达 250 名。

地震发生后不久，英国长老会迅速派出一支赈济队伍赶到南澳岛，成员包括福音医院的医生。他们抵达后就在岛上成立赈济中心，分发药物和救灾物品，并以中心作为临时医院，为伤者提供简单的治疗。根据福音医院的赈灾报告：

> 我们就立即派出两队人员"挨家挨户"看望当地灾民。这时全部灾民

都没有一所像样的房子，用两道木门搭成一个倒转的 V 字，那就是大多数人的避难所。但是我们没有足够的空间让医疗人员进行驳骨手术。一队人进入市集，另一队人则在城外工作……有140名伤者在现场救治，临时医院则处理了250人。

长老会医疗队必须面对林林总总的伤势。他们为伤者处理简单的骨伤，患处包括手、脚、脊柱、胸骨和盆骨，还有10宗骨折个案因为已经出现坏疽必须进行截肢手术。他们不眠不休地工作了至少5天，为每一名伤者提供治疗。当离开南澳岛时，他们已经出动了448次，在临时医院协助处理个案总计778宗。

1922 年的"八二风灾"

1922 年 8 月 2 日在汕头刮起的台风，对赈灾行动带来了巨大的考验。台风挟住海浪横扫位于沿岸低洼地区，卷走了数以百计的人命、牲口和渔船。正如长老会传教士的忆述：

1922 年 8 月 2 日星期三下午，天色异样，山雨欲来，到了午夜终于吹起怪风。台风最初从东北猛烈吹袭了 3 至 5 个钟头，忽然风势静止了大约 30 至 40 分钟，之后从西南方向又刮起风来，大风持续了 5 个钟头 。这样的情况真是糟透了，因为疾风带着海水把岸边的一切摧毁殆尽。

暴风仿佛要将每个生命推向末日的临界点，被大风肆虐的汕头市俨如人间地狱。重返灾区的生还者在沿岸废墟中徘徊，试图寻找失散的亲友和收拾仅存的财物。

英国传教士任杜力解释市内遭受严重破坏的原因：汕头市内大部分街道位于低洼地区，距离水位线不到 3 米。每当海浪高涨，浮在水面的舢板、渔船和电动船受到海水和飓风往来驱动，摧毁防波堤、电灯柱、电线杆，又推倒民房门窗，最后把屋内的生命和财物吞噬。

在汕头郊区，灾情尤其严重。比如澄海盐灶的长老会教会，8 月 2 日当晚数十人死亡，其中一位教会长老一家21口全告身亡。遗体在数天后被发现时全部身穿白袍，一般人以为他们只是在临死前穿上丧服面对死神。然而，白袍是崇拜时穿着的圣礼袍或者诗班袍，而白色在基督教意义上象征洁白无污，正如《圣经·启示录》第7章所描写那样，在最后一刻，这个家庭怀着极大的期盼和信心，全家人穿上白袍等待与他们的救主相遇。悲剧为传教士和信徒说明了信仰的感召，给予他们重建灾区的动力。水退后的汕头海滨一片狼藉，担负起赈灾任务的教会，并未因灾情严重而气馁，反而迅速行动起来，向海外教会寻求援助。

赈灾活动的成功，取决于地方上的配合。盐灶堂的吴国维牧师和其他林姓信徒便是一例。他们除了重建教堂和小区之外，更善用外来的援助成立了一所孤儿院，为村内的孩子提供避难所。

Chapter 4   Christian Disaster Management

A rainbow rises from the sea,

Wind blows from all directions like the heavy rain pouring in the battlefield.

The big green tree in front of the house is uprooted,

Grain crops and water in the fields completely dry up.

People have little left in the granaries by autumn,

People cannot afford to buy clothing by the end of the year.

When opening the window and seeing the blue sky after the typhoon,

People talk about delaying tax payment under the *lijia* system.

Late imperial scholar–official Li Zhi lucidly captured the destructive power of a typhoon in Chaoshan. Throughout history, natural disasters have frequently struck the region. The scope and severity of the disasters badly affected the people, who implored the local gentry and government officials to relieve the disaster–stricken communities. But when the Qing dynasty collapsed in 1911 and the modern state was not yet established, it fell on the shoulders of non–government organizations to undertake relief efforts. This was particularly true for the American Baptist and English Presbyterian missions.

The following photos depict the severe flooding in September 1911, the earthquake on February 13, 1918, and the typhoon on August 2, 1922. These disasters galvanized foreign missionaries, native Christians, local merchants, and officials into action.

Flooding in September 1911

In early September, a month before the outbreak of the Republican Revolution (1911), heavy rain caused floods along the coast of Chaoshan. On September 8 and 9, the downpour overflowed the banks of the lower Han River. Old dams and levees could not hold back floodwaters and the lower Han River region was completely flooded. People who lived along the river banks evacuated to the high ground and camped on the dykes.

On September 11, the missionaries founded the Chaozhou Floods Relief Committee, which reflected a cross-section of both the Chinese and foreign elite in Shantou in a striking display of Sino-Western cooperation. John Campbell Gibson, an English Presbyterian, chaired the committee. The missionaries sent a team of volunteers to inspect the scale of property and human loss in the flooded areas, and relied on a handful of Chinese distributors and local churches to reach out to the victims in the countryside.

The Earthquake on February 13, 1918

Besides seasonal flooding, earthquakes frequently occurred in the Nanpeng archipelago and its adjacent waters, and seriously affected the Chaoshan coast. The most disastrous earthquake took place at 2:07 pm on February 13, 1918. During the earthquake, Frank Foster of the Baptist Mission was crossing the harbor and saw "a cloud of dust over both Swatow [Shantou] and Kakchieh [Queshi]". The American Baptist Mission headquarters, on the hilly slope of Queshi, widely known as Rocky Corner, suffered minor damage. But in Shantou and Nan'ao Island, there were large numbers of casualties. As Lida Scott Ashmore reported,

In Swatow many houses have fallen and as the streets are so narrow, there was no place where they could go to be out of the way of falling walls. Many have been dug out of the ruins. A number of days ago a society which furnishes coffins to those who cannot afford to buy, had given 140 coffins away... Over on Namoa (Nan'ao) Island the chief city is laid low but the report comes that only 250 people are killed.

Shortly after the earthquake, the English Presbyterians sent medical practitioners from the Shantou Gospel Hospital to Nan'ao. Upon arrival, they set up a distribution center to deliver relief supplies and medicine. The center also served as a temporary hospital. According to the Presbyterian relief report,

As soon as the medical supplies had been unpacked, we arranged for two parties to visit the "home" of the people. At this time, no one was living in a house: two doors leaning together like an inverted "V" formed the sort of shelter into which most people crept at night—but these shelters did not leave much room for setting a fracture etc. One party went into the City; the other, outside... Over 140 patients had been treated in their own homes and 250 in the temporary hospital.

The Presbyterian medical team encountered all sorts of injuries among the victims. They treated "simple" fractures in every part of the body—arms, legs, spine, chest and pelvis. There were also ten compound fractures in which gangrene had set in, where amputation was required. The team spent at least five days and nights treating patients. They carried out 448 home visits and assisted with 778 treatments inside the temporary hospital.

The Typhoon on August 2, 1922

The typhoon of August 2, 1922 was a major test of the Christian relief operation in Chaozhou. This typhoon lifted a vast mass of seawater and hurled it on low-lying villages along the entire coastal region, sweeping away countless people, animals, and fishing boats. As the Presbyterian missionaries recalled,

First it [typhoon] came from the northeast and blew furiously for four or five hours; then came a lull of 30 or 40 minutes at midnight, and afterwards the wind rushed in from the southwest, raging for another five hours. The worst feature of it was that it was accompanied by a kind of tidal wave, and as part of the coast was flat, the tidal wave simply overwhelmed everything.

Everyone was frightened by the violence of the storm. The situation in Shantou was indeed disastrous. T. W. Douglas James explained the reasons for the large scale of destruction in Shantou:

Swatow is in many parts barely above high water level and probably no part is more than ten feet over that level. The result was that the tide had swept in using junks, sampans and everything that could float as battering rams and with the help of the wind had knocked down boundary walls, telegraph and telephone and electric light poles, broken in doors and windows on the ground floor of the houses and go-downs and on its retreat had swept out most of the contents....The Bund presented an indescribable scene of wreckage.

Shantou and nearby cities suffered badly, but the plight of the villages was worse. Of all the deaths in Yanzao village in Chenghai district, the most moving was that of an entire Presbyterian family of twenty-one people. When, a few days later, their drowned bodies were found wearing white clothes, many Chinese assumed that the whole family followed the traditional custom of dressing in undyed white garments to express sorrow for each other's death. To Christians, however, the white garments resonated with the religious symbol of purity and righteousness, and more importantly, with the biblical prophecy of rapture or "End Time", in which some chosen believers would purify themselves by dressing in white to meet the returning Jesus Christ in the air (Revelation 7).

The English missionaries witnessed the power of faith that these believers demonstrated at the end of their life. Trapped in a tidal wave, the family saw no escape, as water and mud crashed into their home. Facing the inevitability of death, the Christian patriarch calmly and quickly instructed everyone to put on white garments and prayed to overcome the unbearable pain of dying together. Their final moment was one of tragedy and triumph, and the missionaries and local congregants firmly believed that this family had met the Lord in eternity.

The tidal wave also left sixty orphans, and the Yanzao congregation utilized outside donations to build an orphanage to discourage the kidnap and sale of children by starving refugees. The tragedy of the August 2nd typhoon, thus, became a significant part of the collective memory of Yanzao Christians.

1911 年 9 月潮州水灾后，韩江水位尚未退去
The flooded river banks of Chaozhou City, September 1911

1918 年 2 月 13 日地震后汕头一幢彻底倒塌的楼房。之前的大楼内有商店、餐馆和住房等
What used to be the building housing a shop, a restaurant, and residence...

倒塌楼房的另一角
Another view of the collapsed building

处境与视野：潮汕中外交流的光影记忆

外墙倒塌的洋楼

The exterior walls of this building collapsed after the earthquake

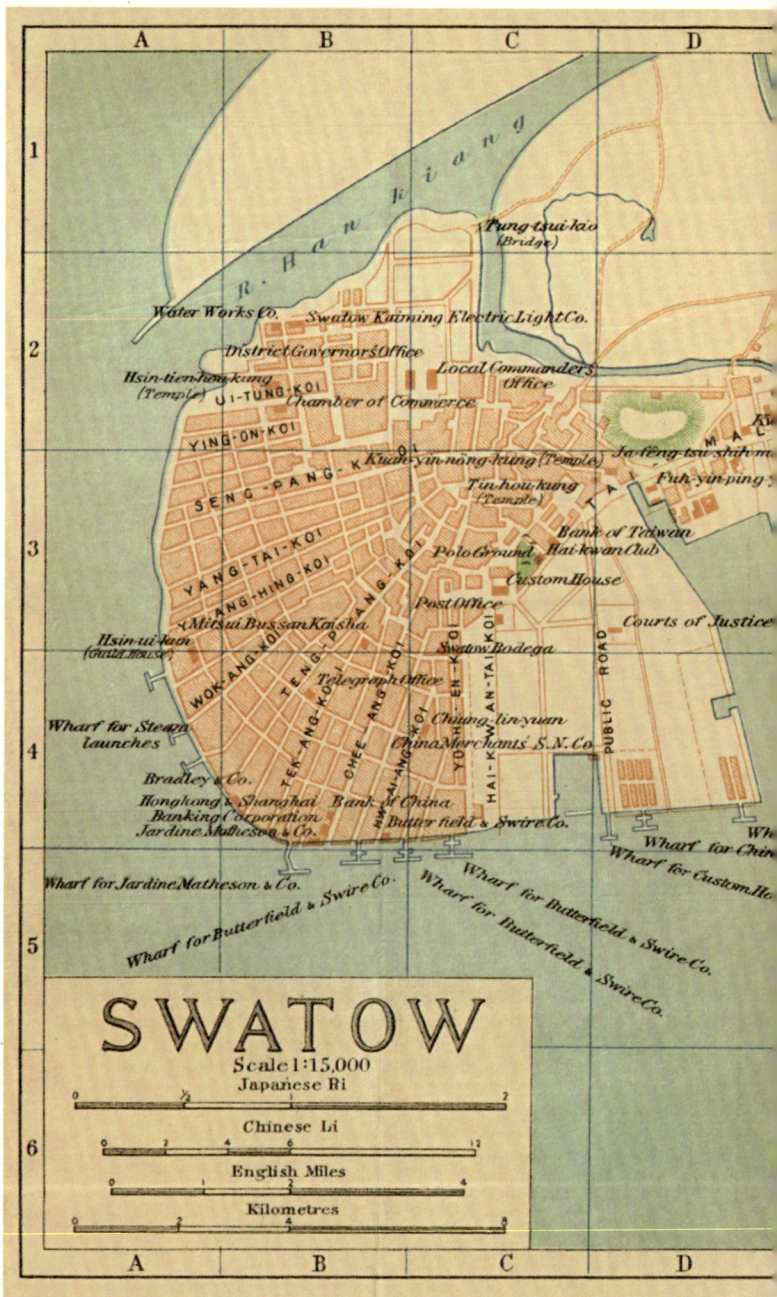

A map fills most of the page. The following labels are visible on the map:

SWATOW

Scale 1:15,000

Japanese Ri

Chinese Li

English Miles

Kilometres

Map labels:

Han Kiang

Tung-tsui-kao (Bridge)

Water Works Co.

Swatow Kaiming Electric Light Co.

District Governor's Office

Local Commanders Office

Hsin-tien-kung-kung (Temple)

Chamber of Commerce

UI-TUNG-KOI

YING-ON-KOI

SENG-PANG-KOI

Kuan-yin-nong-kung (Temple)

Tin-hou-kung (Temple)

Ja-fung-tsu-shatow

Fuh-yin-ping

TAI MALL

YANG-TAI-KOI

ANG-HING-KOI

Polo Ground

Bank of Taiwan

Hai-kwan Club

Custom House

Courts of Justice

Mitsui Bussan Kaisha

Hsin-ui-tan (Guild-house)

Post Office

Swatow Bodega

WOK-ANG-KOI

TEK-ANG-KOI

TENG-PANG-KOI

CHEE-ANG-KOI

KI-ANG-KOI

SHEN-KOI

HAI-PANG-TAI-KOI

YONG-NAM-KOI

PUBLIC ROAD

Telegraph Office

Chung-lin-yuan

China Merchants' S. N. Co.

Wharf for Steam launches

Bradley & Co.

Hongkong & Shanghai Banking Corporation

Bank of China

Jardine Matheson & Co.

Butterfield & Swire Co.

Wharf for Jardine Matheson & Co.

Wharf for Butterfield & Swire Co.

Wharf for Butterfield & Swire Co.

Wharf for Butterfield & Swire Co.

Wharf for China...

Wharf for Custom Ho...

Wharf...

1924 年的汕头地图，图中的码头和货仓在"八二风灾"时全告摧毁

Map of Shantou Harbor in 1924. Most of the wharfs and warehouses were badly damaged in the typhoon on August 2, 1922

E   F   G   H

Chao-chow

Swatow Station   Dock   to Teng-hai   1

Chao-chow & Swatow Railway Co.   2

chool
ub

K I A - L A T   Anglo-chinese College

n Catholic Church   German Consulate
i-laan
Norwegian Consulate   Astor House Hotel

TAI - MA - LO   General Police Office   Swatow Hotel   Tsung-tung-shan

American Consulate   Japanese Consulate
Custom Inspection Office   French Consulate
Club   Bureau of Foreign Affairs   Oil Tank   3

Standard Oil Co.

4

ts & Haesloop
's S.N.Co.

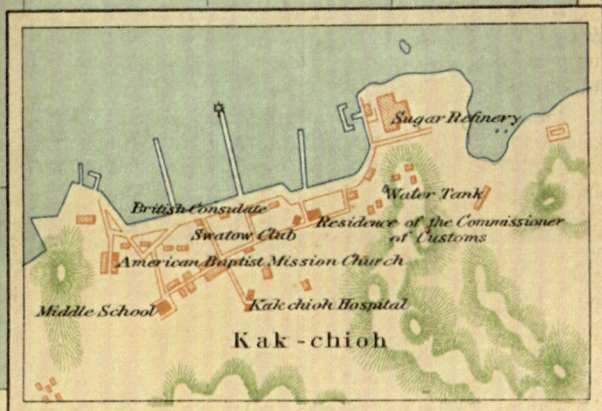

Sugar Refinery

Water Tank
British Consulate   Residence of the Commissioner
Swatow Club   of Customs
American Baptist Mission Church

Middle School   Kak-chioh Hospital

K a k - c h i o h

E

"八二风灾"后的礐石，房顶瓦片被毁，树叶被刮精光
The typhoon destroyed the roofs of most buildings in Queshi and stripped the trees

Typhoon
destruction
August 2
'22

"八二风灾"后，农田被淹，农房破败，仅存大树一棵
Most village houses were badly damaged by the typhoon

暴风肆虐后的汕头
Shantou after the typhoon

油头沿岸码头，人们在废墟中四处搜寻
Rescue workers searched for survivors in the collapsed houses

不敌劲风的大树
Fallen trees

被严重破坏的电灯柱、电线杆，汕头市断电数周。灾民返回灾区寻找失物
Survivors walked past collapsed telegraph, telephone and electric light poles. They had returned to their homes to look for missing relatives

无数坍塌的货仓引致的经济损失难以估量
Collapsed warehouses in Shantou with losses hard to estimate

码头设施被破坏后，导致不少依靠码头维生的工人和苦力失业

Wharfs and warehouses in Shantou were destroyed, and many workers lost their livelihoods

渔船和电动船被吹翻，对当地渔业和运输业造成严重的打击
Overturned boats were everywhere, affecting fisheries and transportation

人们仍期望在倒塌的木屋和棚屋中寻获生还者
People searched for survivors in the collapsed buildings

舢板受到海水和台风往来驱动，摧毁了防波堤
Sampans washed onto the shore

被海水推上岸的渔船和电动船破坏了房屋
Ships washed onto the shore

被推到洋房花园前的电动船

A ship was washed onto a house garden

　处境与视野：潮汕中外交流的光影记忆

风灾后沿岸的废墟
Ruins after the disaster. People desperately looked for their missing relatives and family possessions

码头边上供工人居住的棚屋被台风和大浪卷走，伤亡惨重
All the wooden structures and huts collapsed under the typhoon. People removed dead bodies from the debris

右方是天主教汕头教区主教楼，旁边的小楼损毁严重
A collapsed building next to the 3–story Shantou Catholic Mission Headquarters

天主教汕头教区主教楼，该楼今已不在
The former 3–story Shantou Catholic Mission Headquarters

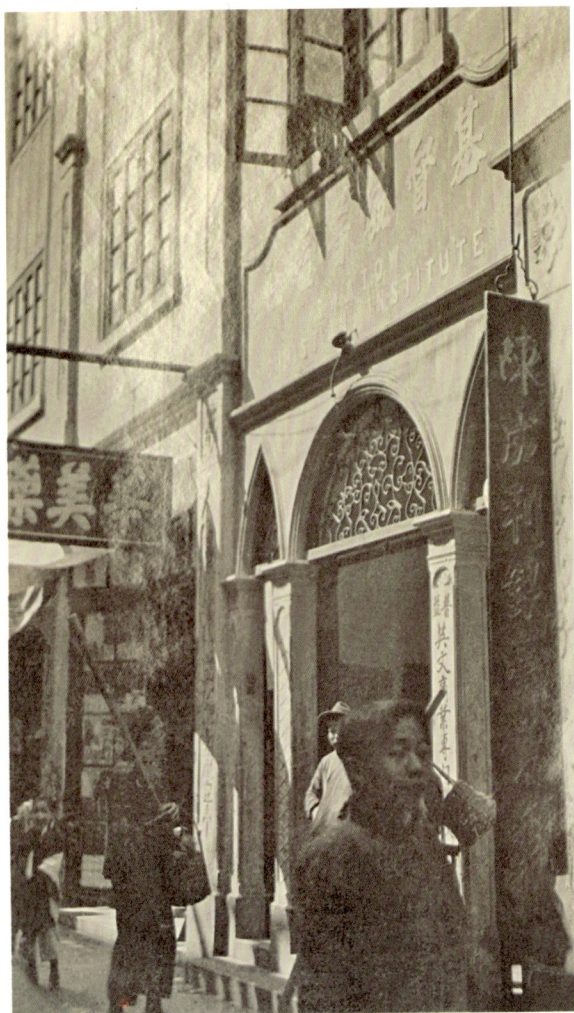

浸信会在汕头镇邦街 68 号的普益社
The Baptist-run Christian Institute in Shantou

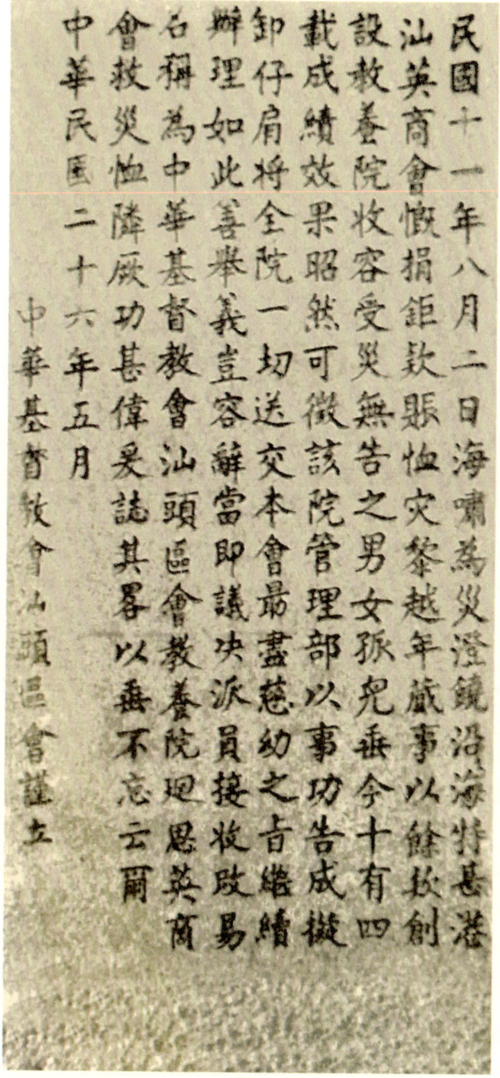

民國十一年八月二日海嘯為災澄鏡沿海特甚潜
汕英商會慨捐鉅欵賑恤災黎越年藏事以餘欵創
設教養院牧容受災無告之男女孤兒垂今十有四
載成績效果昭然可徵該院管理部以事功告成擬
卸仔肩將全院一切送交本會最盡慈幼之吉繼續
辦理如此善舉義壹容辭當即議决派員接收政易
石稱為中華基督教會汕頭區會教養院迎恩英商
會救災恤隣厥功基偉爰誌其畧以垂不忘云爾

中華民國二十六年五月

中華基督教會汕頭區會謹立

盐灶堂立碑纪念"八二风灾"

Commemoration of the August 2nd Typhoon in Yanzao

吴国维牧师史略

牧师揭阳曲溪乡人吴克快公独子生于一八八二年幼聪颖好学作至工神学院毕业後牧师揭阳曲溪乡人吴克快公独子生于一八建堂绩顺任牧职六载一九一九于愿盐灶堂纪念堂以表彰其贡献又大力倡道救会

慨捐巨款建孤儿院一九三六年牧师造一九四三年牧师任职道十七年於汕头退休

餘款建孤儿院特请牧师任职为董事长兼院长又任贝职

任上棉湖联结堂牧师岭东大会理事长怀于一九四八年五月廿八日病天国享寿七十德配夫教子女五各有成就现蒙其晢嗣瑞三君捐资修建此堂

理神学院董事长事会全国基督教长老大会出席全国基督教长牧师任岭东大会理事长能全心全意服务救会师母晚年病天国享寿九十四子四

等职陈氏贤内助故於一九七三年版天家享寿九十四子

塔掃賢一九五八年五月廿八日病天国享

女年表追思

其在卓馨施救遗训爱吴牧功在岭东勤吾後进诚足欽棠安其芳踪

藉发牧师之时致函区会文云维任之日猶才豐学硕撰足致区会文云维离任之日猶

盐灶基督教理事会敬撰
一九八五年十月十日

第五章　道在寻源

　　澄海盐灶教堂大门口上的四个朝廷御赐大字"道在寻源"，标志着第一代潮汕信徒热切求道的宗教情怀。潮汕基督教是十分本土化的宗教，19世纪晚期的大部分潮汕信徒并不是生活在汕头的买办精英，而是身居乡村、朝夕耕作的普通村民。

　　信徒与传教士携手建立教堂，这在昔日的社会具有十分重大的意义。教堂成了祠堂、寺庙以外的神圣场所；通过在教堂举行的崇拜活动、《圣经》研习、唱诗祈祷和圣餐聚会，地方上出现了崭新的宗教生活。教会环境的熏陶不断培育出新一代的信徒和教会领袖，使其信仰得以代代相传。

　　创办教堂的第一代信徒往往来自地方宗族，他们会整个家庭，甚至全支族派加入教会。这种集体入教的现象，在当时的潮汕地区非常普遍。第一代长辈成了信徒家族的新祖先，基督教信仰成了家族的新身份认同，他们编写基督徒族谱，采用基督化的婚丧礼仪，并实行教内通婚。

　　本章照片展示的是潮汕内陆的教堂建筑、教会崇拜和布道用的印刷品以及信徒家庭的合影，从中可见基督教逐步融入乡土社会的痕迹。

　　盐灶堂是长老会在潮汕地区最早的教堂。早在1847年，瑞士巴色会传教士黎力基最先被派到当地工作。盐灶是个杂姓社区，四个村落分别是上社、上厝、中社和港头。上社和中社居住了刘、蔡、李姓宗族；而上厝和港头分别由林氏宗族的长房和次房控制。英国长老会在盐灶的发展，与港头林氏宗族次房关系密切。黎力基在澄海五年的岁月里，把福音传给港头林氏次房。林旗是第一批信徒之一，他在1861年邀请了英国长老会的宾为邻到盐灶扩展教务。

盐灶长老会创立之初，教堂建筑甚为简朴。正如第一代乡村教堂大多由民房改建一样，盐灶教堂楼顶没有十字架，门楣上"礼拜堂"三个大字是基督教的唯一标志。随着时间的推移，盐灶堂成了澄海、饶平两县边境的乡村教会中心。在19世纪60年代，从盐灶堂发展出仙洲、浮山和黄冈三个长老会教堂。地方信徒在二十多年间，把盐灶乡从一个不知名的村子变成了潮汕基督教的重镇。

类似的情况也发生在笔者先父李松添的故乡。汕头市古溪村是一条寨墙环绕、小河环抱的围村。南宋年间建村时，先民因缺乏水源而开凿溪道，后人为纪念祖先功绩，遂取村名为"苦溪"，后雅称"古溪"。今日古溪村由郭、李、姚、郑等宗族组成。在美北浸信会和法国天主教巴黎外方传道会到来之前，村民都是烧香拜庙。19世纪末，李氏宗族的两房分别加入浸信会和天主教会。自从基督新教和天主教进入古溪村之后，教会和当地的宗族结构融为一体，成为村民自我身份认同的重要部分之一。

盐灶和古溪信徒群体的相同之处可见于照片。影像中的旧教堂、村落围墙和望楼建筑，告诉我们基督教运动的活动处境，显示出西方传教士和信徒将福音融入地方社会的开放务实取向。信徒的墓碑则清楚地显示了他们的信仰身份，比如新教信徒的墓碑上刻有十字架并注明"基督门徒"字样，而天主教徒墓碑则刻上墓主的圣名（即教名）。

最后，本章所展示的汕头土白话《圣经》和诗歌集，说明了中外文化交流过程中所带来的珍贵物质遗产，为当地人民吸收外来知识提供了有效的工具，在学习的过程中又达到扫盲和提升国人文化水平的效果。

Chapter 5 Seeking the Way

When the Presbyterians in Yanzao, Chenghai district decorated their chapel's entrance with a tablet, "Dao zai xun yuan (The Way is to seek the origin)", they revealed their religious fervor and their determination to practice the faith. Once global Christianity rooted itself in Chaoshan as a truly indigenous religion through the Christianization of family genealogies and lineage networks, native congregations acquired a level of autonomy which permitted a greater role for faith—based institutions in community governance.

In late nineteenth—century Chaoshan, the countryside was the center of the Christian missionary movement and a typical Chinese believer was a man or woman living in a densely—populated village. Christianity was integrated into the preexisting kinship and lineage structures and grew as a grassroots movement in which Christians succeeded in recruiting converts, building churches, accommodating their faith with traditional customs, and developing social and religious bonds. This networking effect contributed to the process of Christianization, as the gospel passed from individual to individual, family to family, village to village.

This chapter draws on photos that illustrate the gradual integration of Christianity into the Chaoshan lineage society. The best example of this integration is the Presbyterian movement in Yanzao. Founded in 1849, the Yanzao church was the oldest Presbyterian congregation in Chaoshan. As a multi—lineage community, Yanzao has four territorial settlements, namely Shangshe (Upper Shrine), Shangcuo (Upper Village), Zhongshe (Middle Shrine), and Gangtou (Sea Port). Whereas Shangshe and Zhongshe were settled by the Liu, Cai, and Li lineages, Shangcuo and Gangtou were the strongholds of the senior and junior segments of the Lin lineage, respectively.

The Presbyterian expansion into Yanzao was related to the rise of the junior Lin segments in Gangtou. Rudolf Lechler of the German Basel Mission came to Chaoshan in 1847. Before leaving for Hong Kong in 1852, Lechler converted several members of the junior Lin segment, including Lin Qi. It was Lin Qi who asked William Chalmers Burns of the English Presbyterian Mission to visit Yanzao in 1861.

After the founding of the Presbyterian congregation in Yanzao, Lin Qi became the church leader and received much help from the missionaries to administer the chapel. Yanzao's church soon became the largest congregation along the border of Chenghai and Raoping districts.

A similar example of collective conversion can be seen in my late father's ancestral home in Chaoyang district. As a walled village surrounded by a river, Kuxi (River of Hardship) is composed of the Guo, Li, Yao and Zheng lineages. Prior to the arrival of Baptist Christianity and Catholicism, the people of this multi—lineage community were temple worshippers. In the late nineteenth century, two segments of the Li lineage joined the Baptist and Catholic churches, respectively. The capacity of Christianity to merge with local cultures and kinship networks strengthened the foundation of the Kuxi churches.

As shown in the photos, most Chaoshan Christians combined the Western denominational structure with local kinship, village, and lineage networks. This fascinating process of cross—cultural interaction reveals the frequent crossovers of new and old identities in the lives of these Christians. For example, the

Yanzao Presbyterians founded a Christian cemetery on Lotus Hill, assuring the congregants that their tombs were surrounded by those of their relatives and friends. They revered their ancestors by holding special church services and visiting their graves every spring. The tombstones referred to the first converts as "disciples of Christ" (*Jidu mentu*), expressing the religious identity and pride of the deceased. Through these diversified linkages between the Gospel and Chinese *guanxi*, we can appreciate the indigeneity of Chaoshan Christianity.

In addition, translation and indigenization go hand in hand in the spread of Christianity. The momentum of Christianity as a world religion lies in the ability to transmit its core message and take roots in any cross–cultural settings. What speaks about the linguistic aspect of this momentum is the collaboration between Chaoshan Christians and foreign missionaries in producing vernacular materials such as the Bible, religious tracts, and hymnals for evangelization. Many Chaozhou readers found the Christian message to be familiar because it was conveyed in their native tongue, and the Christian God to be approachable because He was thought to communicate with them in the same language.

长老会盐灶教堂第一张照片，大门口上"道在寻源"四个大字，标志着第一代潮汕信徒的宗教情怀。成人前数第二排左起第七位为林旗

The first group photo of the Yanzao Presbyterian congregation

民国时期的盐灶乡长老会教堂
The Yanzao Presbyterian Church in the Republican Era

盐灶教堂至今是村内最高建筑物之一，这是从教堂顶上俯瞰盐灶乡一角
A view of Yanzao

处境与视野：潮汕中外交流的光影记忆

经盐灶堂教友修缮的清末第一代信徒之墓

Several newly–decorated tombstones of late–nineteenth–century Yanzao Christians

浸信会在潮州市所建办的教堂，门的两旁以福音对联装饰
A modest Baptist church in Chaozhou City

昔日葛州浸信会老教堂已不复存在，刻有"礼拜堂"三个大字的
大石块，因为坚固质优而侥幸得以保存，被用作小巷建筑
The old stone tablet of the Gezhou Baptist Church

大门口上"礼拜堂"三个大字把一所普通民房变成崇拜场所。位于潮阳古溪村寨内的老教堂，原是李氏信徒一家的住屋，于 1880 年供礼拜使用

The first Baptist chapel was erected inside the walled village of Kuxi in 1880

古溪信徒于 1946 年在村寨外兴建的新教堂，今已不在
A larger Baptist church was built outside the walled village of Kuxi to celebrate the end of World War Ⅱ in 1946

古溪天主教教堂
The Kuxi Catholic Church Compound

古溪天主教教堂旁的钟楼，楼身
全部以十字架装饰
**The Kuxi Catholic Church Bell
Tower**

1923 年潮州城内的天主教教堂，钟楼的设立使之成为城内的最高建筑物
The Catholic Church in Chaozhou City in 1923

1930 年浸信会建于礐石的教堂，外观为中式建筑风格，其用料和教堂大钟则是从美国进口
The Baptist Church in Queshi

1923 年浸信会教堂内挂上各国国旗，象征福音传遍天下
The Baptist Church's interior in 1923

1937 年以前，浸信会举行差传宣教周，以英语介绍各地的宣教工作，其中特别提到汕头地区的
教会学校和门徒训练
A Baptist missionary exhibition in Shantou

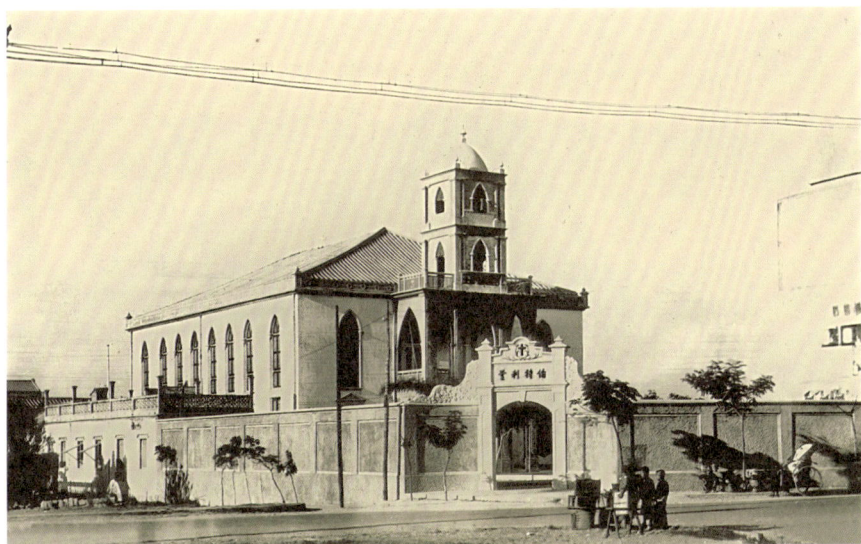

建于 1928 年的汕头长老会伯特利教堂
The Bethel Church in Shantou was founded in 1928

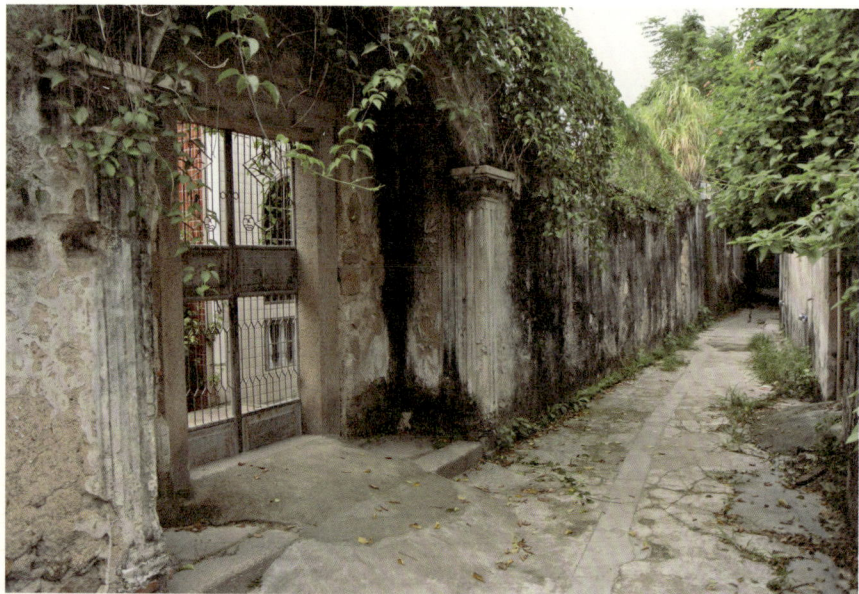

昔日旧溪东教堂旁的老围墙，糅合了西洋特色的石柱尚隐约可见
An old house wall near the Xidong Church

信徒在阅读宗教读物
Christian printing

論真神

世上有一位神名叫耶和華。伊昔在今在終久在伊是無起頭亦無終尾。未有天地未有人物先有這一位神伊時時在處處在件件能件件理天地萬物是伊創造的。天中的日頭月娘星宿件件是伊造的地上的山海溪河各件亦是伊造的山頂的禽獸昆蟲海底的魚蝦龜鱉亦是伊造的草木蔬菜菓子五穀麻豆蔘參亦是伊發生給人食世上的物不論是甚麼物都是伊造的。伊是天地人物的主天是伊的地是伊的脚踏的物。伊出日飄風落雨雷轟落露○伊是世上人的始祖公伊是生命的源頭人生人死是伊主意伊知人的事不論日間夜間伊都看見人暗靜做的事伊亦知心内想的伊亦知○人亦是行善伊就惜伊保佑伊賞伊人亦是做惡伊就追責伊刑罰伊○這位神是天下萬國人相共的天上下無別個神好拜這位神○伊主意亦知人的欲拜這位真活的神亦免插香亦免燒紙亦免奉物亦免入宮廟去拜○這一位意來服事伊順伊的命聽伊的律例改惡從善○這一位活神使有一個救世主在這世間贖人的罪救人的靈魂相信神使有一個救世主在這世間贖人的罪救人的靈魂正能得到天堂。

論死後的事

人死後單單有二處好去一處是悽慘的一處是快活的悽慘的叫做地獄快活的叫做天堂地獄内是暗暗入去的彼火終久燒彼蟲終久咬與魔鬼惡人一同居住一人在那裏就不得再出來○人若是相信福音道理順救主的命令死後就到天堂在彼處衆人是歡喜快樂彼處的路是金的屋是玉的終久不能廢壞彼處的人穿白衫哩終久清潔彼處的地方不寒不熱無蚊無虱是終久光全不暗彼處的人免曝日免淋雨不生病不死免艱苦免煩惱免流目汁不喉渴不肚飢不貧窮到彼處瞎眼的目睭就光且聾聵就能聽話啞就能講話廢疾的人廢疾就能好癲瘋的人癲瘋就能好彼處無人相罵相打相惡恨人人相惜一同安安樂樂同心同意拜真活的神彼處惡人魔鬼不得入去彼處的地方是救主做皇帝的伊的門徒共伊一同在人到彼處就是終久在彼處免再來遠世間到天堂的事是萬萬年有福氣○世間的事是幾十年的事死後的事是萬萬年的事在這世間刻苦忍耐勿想着艱苦應該相信救主學伊的榜從伊的規矩到死後能得到天堂就好

以潮州方言写成的福音单张《论真神》《论死后的事》

Christian pamphlets on "True God" and "Life after Death", written in Chaozhou dialect

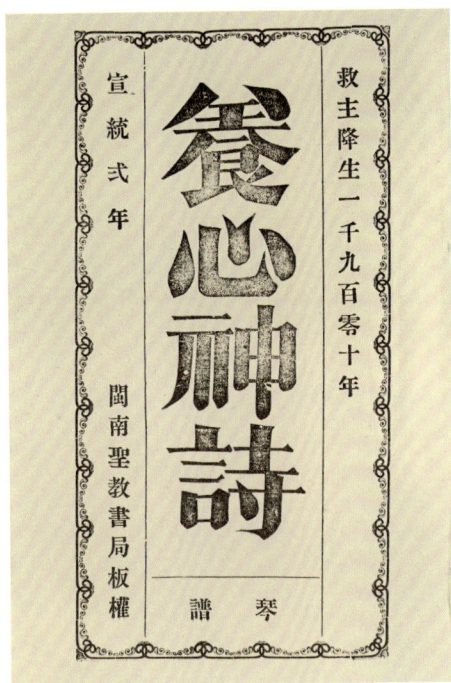

救主降生一千九百零十年

養心神詩

宣統弍年

閩南聖教書局板權

琴譜

1910 年出版的潮语《养心神诗》及琴谱

A Chaozhou Christian hymnal printed in 1910

養心神詩序

養心神詩之作也原爲禮拜堂敬拜上帝仰吾儕及期頌吟講謝上帝之恩
以表明服事者之誠心實意耳但前日舊本雖有傳教而誦讀之下難如人
僅識其字終不能得其義夫既不得其義則其中有所包含意思皆未足通
曉故仍本其義而以白話土腔關明其意思又增以幾首庶幾此後按期敬
拜者吟諸口自可悟於心聆諸耳亦能會其義如保羅所謂吾將以神新禱
亦必使人明吾意將以神頌詩亦必使人達吾意所患者土腔白話未免無
字爲多由是於無字之姑用正字借其字義以代邊加小圈爲別讀者若遇無
圈字就字讀字若無圈者將字解說白話吟下音韻自無不叶且其登堂禮
拜何患口吟而心不悟耳聽而意不會哉抑以見頌祝上帝之恩爲有實焉
叙此以聞

此序言解释重印《养心神诗》的缘由，是为了让潮汕信徒能够用母语歌颂和敬拜上帝，并且明白诗歌歌词的意义

A preface to the 1910 edition of the Chaozhou Christian hymnal

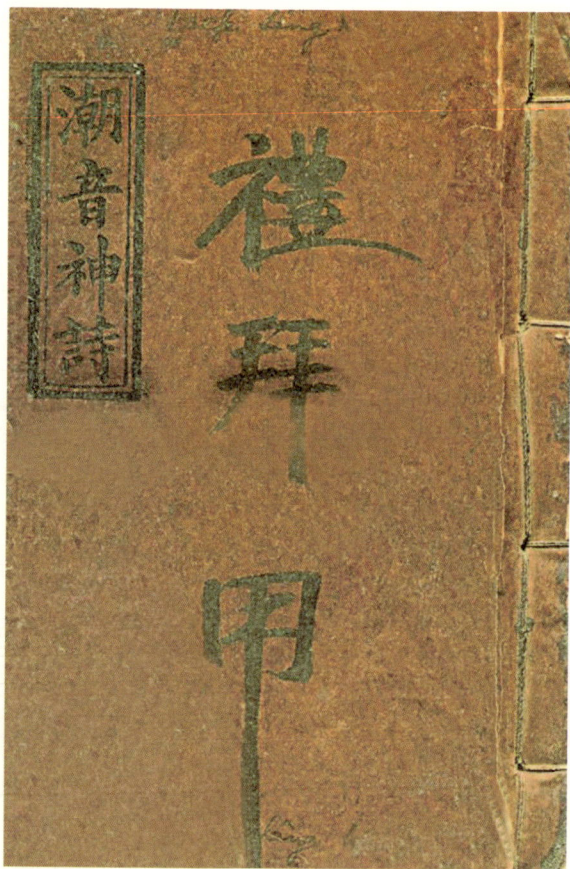

宾为怜于 1861 年编印首部潮语圣诗《潮音神诗》。图为 1923 年
再版之书，为教堂公物

A 1923 reprint of the 1861 edition of William Chalmers Burns'
Chaozhou hymnal

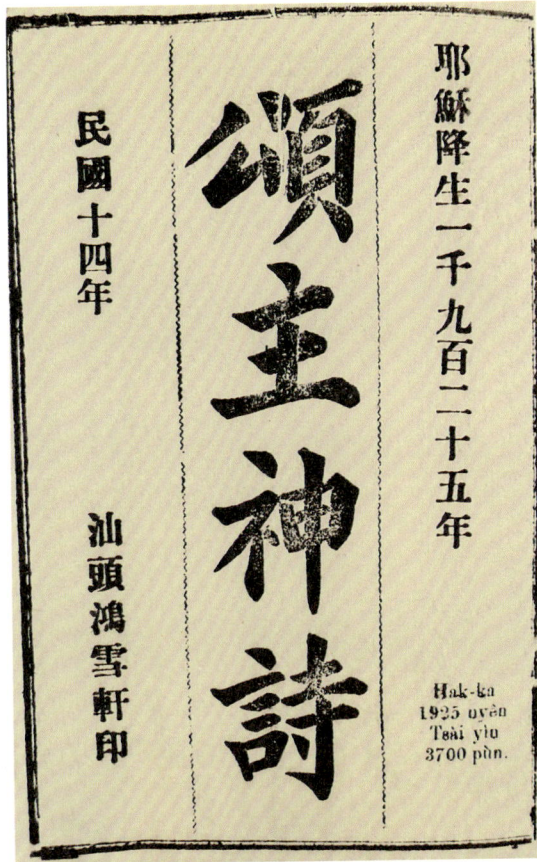

耶穌降生一千九百二十五年

民國十四年

頌主神詩

汕頭鴻雪軒印

Hak-ka
1925 oyen
Tshi yiu
3700 pùn.

1925 年汕头长老会鸿雪轩出版社印发的客语《颂主神诗》
A Hakka–language Presbyterian hymnal printed in 1925

序

夫以吾人受上帝造生保養之恩拯救扶持之德而欲報于萬一則必賴詩以頌讚焉而詩可動人心志發人性情故凡喜怒哀樂之事蓄積於中而發爲言辭歌詠者代不乏人卽古來敬虔之士著爲詩歌載諸舊約新約者莫不本性情心志感激頌揚於是教會自昔迄今每逢安息聖日與夫會集禮拜祈禱之時無不敬誦詩歌同聲唱和一則讚美上帝一則藉養心神本會向用潮音神詩惟因聲韻與客音峭峙致吟誦之際多有不順不能無憾爰復博采各善本中擇其尤佳者重加刪改俾近客音依次編纂爲本教會所用名曰頌主神詩語不求乎工整詞必取乎淺近蓋意義爲重詞藻爲輕不敢以詞害意惟期達聖經之實義庶幾婦孺咸知老幼共曉蒸蒸日上同歸薰陶也願吟是詩者寓以神毋徒富以口各存讚美養心之實意也幸焉是爲序

此序解释了出版缘由，因为方言的分歧，同属长老会的客家信徒感到潮语版的圣诗未能满足他们的信仰需要，因此编制了客语《颂主神诗》

A preface to a Hakka–language Presbyterian hymnal

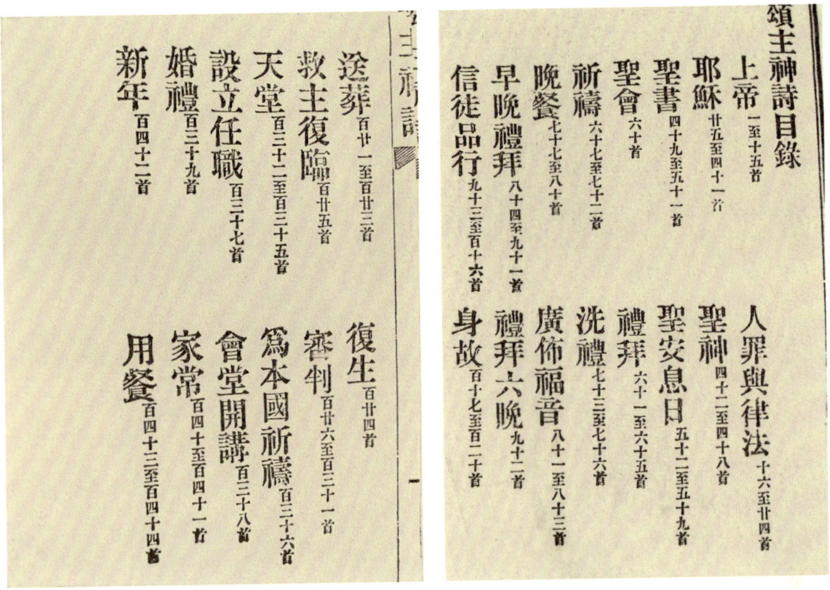

頌主神詩目錄

上帝 一至十五首

人罪與律法 十六至廿四首

耶穌 廿五至四十一首

聖神 四十二至四十八首

聖書 四十九至五十一首

聖安息日 五十二至五十九首

聖會 六十首

禮拜 六十一至六十五首

祈禱 六十一至六十二首

洗禮 七十三至七十六首

晚餐 七十七至八十首

廣佈福音 八十一至八十三首

早晚禮拜 八十四至九十一首

禮拜六晚 九十二首

信徒品行 九十三至百十六首

身故 百十七至百二十首

送葬 百廿一至百廿三首

復生 百廿四首

教主復臨 百廿五首

審判 百廿六至百三十一首

天堂 百三十二至百三十五首

爲本國祈禱 百三十六首

設立任職 百三十七首

會堂開講 百三十八首

婚禮 百三十九首

家常 百四十至百四十一首

新年 百四十二首

用餐 百四十三至百四十四首

客语《颂主神诗》的目录
Hakka hymnal's table of contents

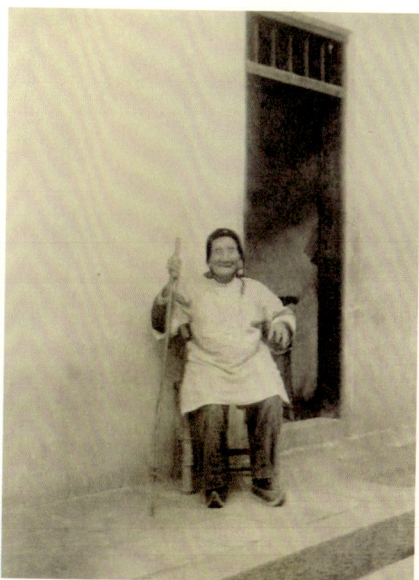

(Miss Probst)   15
                                 5/3
shòi pak-me.
Our first women
member - aged
92.
At first she and
her husband walk-
ed 21 miles (42
altogether) to service
each week.
                    Wukingfu

客语地区五经富第一位女信徒，这是照片及其背面。拍摄这张照片时她已经 92 岁，传教士忆述，她和丈夫每周日徒步 21 公里到长老会教堂聚会。黎明前启程，翻山越岭来到教堂听道，午饭小休后继续聚会，下午日落前起程回家，这是那个时代居于偏远山区信徒的寻道写照

This elderly woman was the first convert at the Hakka-speaking Presbyterian Church in Wujingfu

一位信主妇女
A Christian woman

浸信会传教士陆亚当牧师在 20 世纪 20 年代来到潮州城外的农村施浸，当天站在中间的这位 82 岁的男长者准备接受全身入水的浸礼。当时浸礼在村外河溪中进行，由于是公开的宗教仪式，因此除了教友和受浸者亲朋好友之外，还吸引了大批围观者

American missionary Adam Groesbeck baptized this 82-year-old convert in a village outside Chaozhou City. The baptism attracted many curious onlookers

当地赌博者是传教士经常规劝的对象
Missionaries always reached out to local gamblers and hoped to bring them to the Church

潮汕长老会第一位牧师——陈树铨牧师全家合影

The family photo of the first Presbyterian ordained pastor in Chaoshan

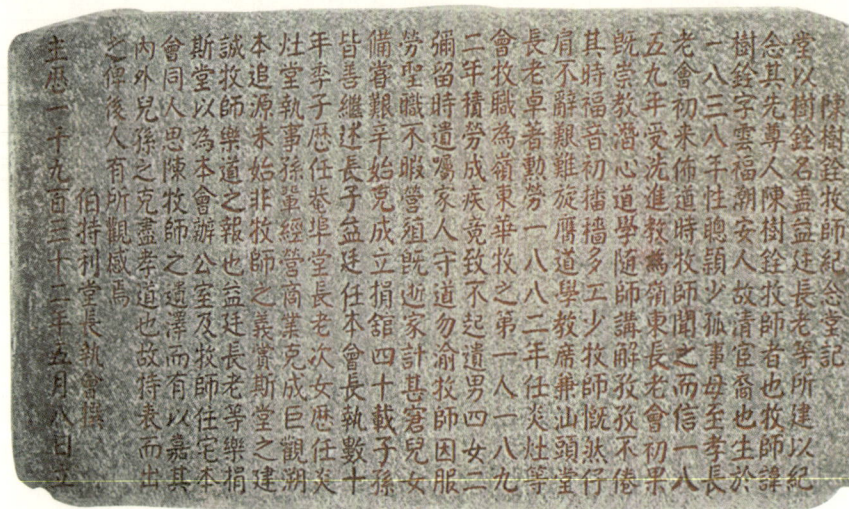

陳樹銓牧師紀念堂記

念堂以其先尊人陳樹銓名盖益廷長老等所建師以紀
一樹銓八字雲三八年性聰穎少孤事母至孝長於譯
五九年初來汕道時進學隨師講解而信景八
老會初受洗道學師長老會初
既崇教音初潛心道學播多工教席兼汕頭堂等
其不辭艱難旋履險阻
肩特福音艱難旋
長老職為嶺東華
二年積勞成疾竟致不起遺男四女二九
會救職甚篤因女服
聖職不暇營家人守道勿逾家計甚篤
彌留時遺囑家人
備嘗艱辛始克成立捐館四十載數子孫
年季子歷任卓埠堂商業
本堂執事堂長老次女
灶子繼述長子益廷任本會次
追源未始非牧師之義賞克成巨觀朔炎十
誠本堂執事堂長老等所建師本捐
斯堂以為本會辦之公至廷牧師老等樂
內同人思之克盡孝道達澤而有表
會外兒孫有所瞻感高堂長執等撰
之碑後人有所瞻感高堂長執等撰而立

主懷一千九百三十二年五月八日立

今存于汕头教会内的清末牧师陈树铨生平纪念碑

The biography of the first Presbyterian ordained pastor in Chaoshan

潮汕长老会第一批教会领袖，前坐右边三位为牧师，其中右二为林旗
A group of Presbyterian preachers and elders in Chaoshan

长老会一位年轻传道人的家庭合影
A young Presbyterian preacher and his family

汕尾长老会教堂的落成典礼
The opening of the Shanwei Presbyterian Church

长老会兰大卫牧师，汕尾教区拓荒者，毕生贡献于当地教会、基督教学校和教会医院

Rev. David Sunderland was the founder of the Presbyterian Mission in Shanwei

1947 年举行的兰大卫牧师追思礼拜
Commemoration of the Rev. David Sunderland of the Shanwei Presbyterian Church

长老会合影
Group photo of missionaries in Wujingfu

玛丽·汤姆逊女士摄于揭西县五经富镇
Female missionary Marie Thomson, the photo was taken in Wujingfu

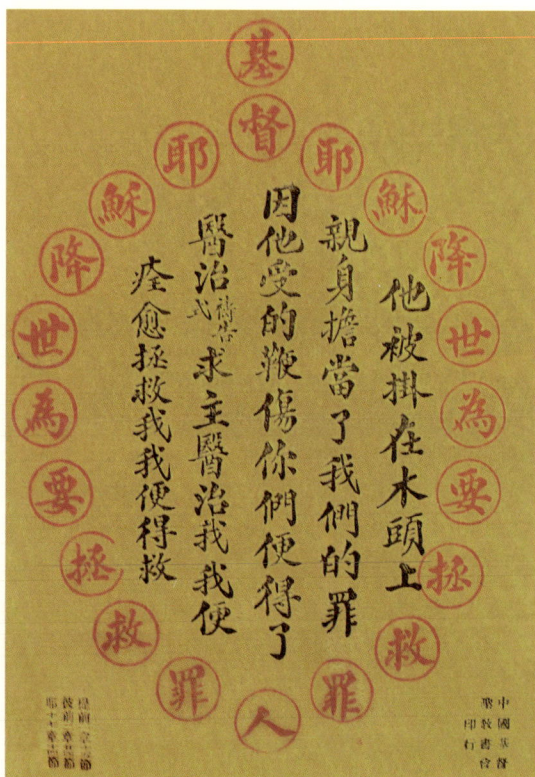

传教单张
Chinese Christian pamphlet

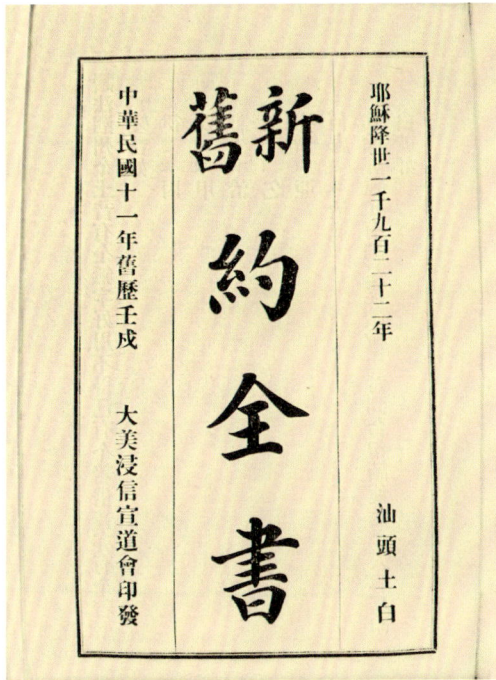

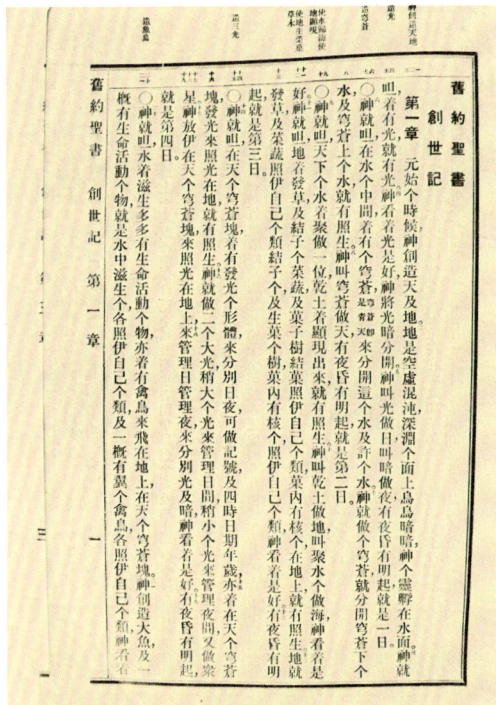

糅合了汕头土话和近代白话的 1922 年版《新旧约全书》，当中的《创世记》以汕头土话"元始个时候"来形容白话的"起初"

The Genesis, Chapter 1, Swatow Old Testament, 1922 Edition

耶琳夫人自编的潮语西乐教材《乐法启蒙》，1893 年出版
Swatow Music Textbook by Lida Scott Ashmore, 1893 Edition

第六章　文化相融

　　本影集的最后一章将带我们回顾潮汕地区中外文化相融的点滴，尤其是基督教文明对潮汕教育、医疗、宗教的正面影响。穿华服、说华语的西方传教士一般被誉为中西文化交流的桥梁。但传教运动所带来的文化交流，并不局限于学贯中西的精英；普通信徒、教会学校学生、与传教士来往的商人都曾参与其中。

　　信徒结合了中外特色的婚嫁喜庆为潮汕社会的文化风俗注入了新元素，表现出中国人对西洋事物的接受和将外来文化嫁植于本地土壤的作风。除了人生仪式之外，日常的衣着发式和人际交往也反映了这种开放的态度。

　　20 世纪 20 年代初在河婆浸信会举行了一场婚礼，其仪式有别于传统的中国婚礼。首先，它是在教堂内进行的，出席者除了一对新人的亲属之外，还有传教士和教友。新郎、新娘穿着糅合了中西特色的礼服。新郎头戴西洋帽子，身着马褂，手持《圣经》；新娘则手握西洋花束，身穿绣花褶裙，脚穿高跟鞋。二人严肃的表情述说了婚礼的庄严和神圣。在牧师的祝福和全体会众的见证之下，他们结为夫妇。牧师特别向他们陈说了基督教的婚姻盟誓，即今后二人要至死不渝地彼此相爱，在地上努力建立一个基督化家庭。礼成后，大家到教堂外的院子中聚餐并拍照留念。类似的婚礼在城市和乡村教会的第二代信徒之间相当普遍。

　　传教士是跨宗教文化的大使，耶琳夫人（1852—1934）就是一例。她和丈夫耶琳牧师（1851—1937）毕生贡献于潮汕教会。耶琳夫人在潮汕的生活体验十分丰富，她的一本册子充分反映了这一点。册子中有她的户外写生、教会学校学生赠送的素描、潮剧表演宣传印刷品、教会信徒赠送的圣诞新年贺卡、商人朋友的名片以及鞭炮包装纸等。

与其他传教士的妻子一样，耶琳夫人经常与丈夫一同下乡布道，她画笔下的河溪渔船和秋收农作物，见证了她对潮汕乡土风情的细腻观察。看潮剧与放鞭炮是潮汕的普遍习俗。昔日的潮剧并不是独立存在的艺术表演形式，潮剧和鞭炮都与民间庙会和宗族活动分不开。下乡布道的传教士经常会碰到迎神赛会，故此他们对潮剧和鞭炮不会感到陌生。他们欣赏潮剧所传达的道德精神和艺术色彩。对一般老百姓而言，鞭炮有驱邪迎新的文化意义，但教会却没有因此而排斥放鞭炮。举办新教堂落成典礼、教会学校奠基典礼、信徒婚礼时，都会响起鞭炮之声。

从开设通商口岸的年代起，通过互换卡片来传递个人信息的西方作风，广泛被地方商人和传道人所采用。耶琳夫人所收集的潮汕商人和朋友的名片，反映了跨文化的友好交往。而在圣诞和元旦自制并互赠贺卡，既表达宗教情谊，也是中国人珍情重礼的实践。

环顾当今全球化和地方化的发展趋势，本影集以潮汕传教士与平民百姓的日常接触为焦点，借此了解西方文化融入中国民间社会的一貌。过去英美汉学界的主流观点，总是倾向于将西方文明与中国社会相遇解释为儒家文化与基督教文化的冲突。在这种学术框架之下，学者将两种文化的交流过程简化为接受或者排斥。其问题就在于只注意了文化精英的反应，而忽略了基层社会在经历外来文化时所产生的变迁。

事实上，西方物质和精神文明在潮汕经历了极为本土化的过程。从教会办学、施医赠药、赈灾施善等方面可见，潮汕人并没有排斥也并非被动地接纳西方事物。他们与传教士一样是这个跨文化融合过程中的先锋，其成功要归因于潮汕人对新事物、新思想永远保持着开放和包容态度的海洋文化传统。近代科学知识和基督教信仰从最初人传人和村传村的模式，发展到日后代代相传，并且建立了众多以服务当地社会为本的学校、医院、教会，都是这种态度的具体写照。这一发展历程，也彻底反驳了西方文明与中国传统文化无法兼容的论点。而本影集所诉说的故事，正为这个论点提供了一个光与影的具体见证。

Chapter 6　Cultural Accommodation

This final chapter revisits the broader theme of cross–cultural interaction in Chaoshan. Scholarship on the history of Chinese–Western cultural encounters still tends to assume that the pronouncements of the small band of foreign missionaries and educated native Christians were representative of the Chinese Christian community as a whole. But the missionary photos show that both Chinese and foreigners were actively involved in the process of material and cultural exchange.

The first two photos show a cosmopolitan Christian wedding that took place in the Baptist church in Hepo in the early 1920s. An eclectic mixture of clothing styles were displayed by the married couple. The wedding service was obviously Christian, but the bride and groom were dressed in different styles. The bride wore a Western–style wedding veil and held flowers. Her attire appeared to be an approximation of Western–style wedding dress. The groom was dressed in typical Chinese clothing as everyone else was in the second photo, and carried a copy of the Bible. The localization of a Christian wedding in an inland river market church lent a cosmopolitan air to the local cultural scene.

Lida Scot Ashmore (1852–1934), wife of Baptist missionary William Ashmore (1851–1937), was another shining example of promoting cross–cultural understanding. She and her husband spent decades living in Chaoshan. In an unpublished scrapbook, Lida preserved many colorful segments of her everyday cross-cultural experience in Shantou including oil paintings, sketches by her students, Chinese religious prints, Christmas cards, business cards of senior political and economic figures, and colored advertisements. These visual materials symbolized her efforts to come to grips with the Chaoshan social customs and practices, and to reconcile cultural differences between East and West. She clearly embraced a new identity as an indigenized American resident in Chaoshan.

In short, these Chaoshan missionary photographs throw light on the ongoing debate about the incompatibility between Chinese and Western culture. The dominant view in Western Sinology has always been concerned with the high culture of China and tends to conceptualize the Chinese-Western cultural encounters as the clash of Confucianism and Christianity. This concept has a tendency to characterize the whole process of cross-cultural interaction as either acceptance or rejection. The problem with this frame of mind is that people beyond the margins of high culture are given no place at all.

In fact, the Chinese-Western cultural encounter turned out to be more smooth and successful than has been acknowledged in the literature. The Chaoshan people were willing recipients of Western material and cultural goods. In partnership with foreign missionaries, they were principal cultural mediators in this development, and were keen to appropriate modern knowledge, skills, and institutions to empower themselves and move up the social ladder. What contributed to this success was the strong maritime tradition of Chaoshan society. In this open and tolerant environment, both modern science and Christian teachings were transmitted from individuals to individuals, families to families, communities to communities. Chaoshan natives did not keep their newfound knowledge to themselves but shared it with others and built many educational, medical and religious institutions to modernize the local society. Their stories reject the outdated thesis of incompatibility between Chinese tradition and Western culture. Only by looking at the photos of these humble cultural mediators can we acquire a better understanding of the dynamics of cosmopolitanism in Chaoshan.

20 世纪 20 年代初河婆浸信会教堂的一对新人，在陆亚当牧师的
祝福下结为夫妇
American missionary Adam Groesbeck blessed this couple in a
Christian wedding in Hepo during the early 1920s

河婆教堂内进行的婚礼
A Christian wedding in the Hepo Baptist Church

民国时期长老会女校毕业生，洋伞和公文包凸显了她的时代气质
A modern Presbyterian woman graduate

耶琳夫人
Lida Scott Ashmore

处境与视野：潮汕中外交流的光影记忆

耶琳牧师与耶琳夫人
William Ashmore Jr. and Lida Scott Ashmore

耶琳夫人的油画观察细腻，除了山丘、河溪、小帆船之外，她还注意到山上的坟墓
A boat and a grove

耶琳夫人的一幅静物写生，画中龙眼为潮汕特产之一
Dragon eye, a popular fruit in Chaoshan

耶琳夫人所收藏的学生写生作品,她经常下乡探
访教会,不会对画中景物感到陌生
Drawings by Lida Scott Ashmore's students

潮剧宣传品，主题分别为"雄阔海打虎"和"秦琼救李渊"
Chaozhou opera pamphlets

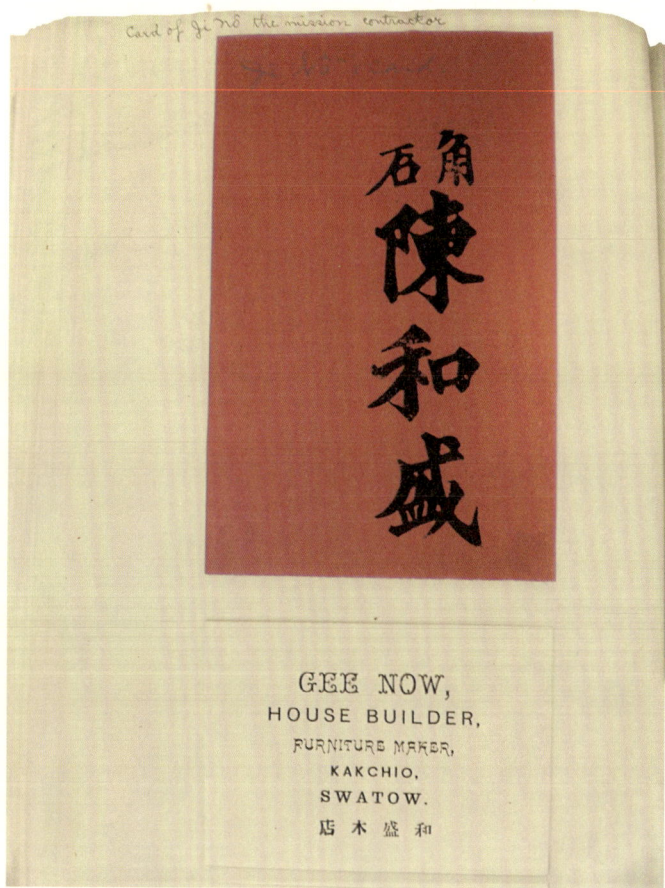

经常受雇于礐石教会的木匠陈和盛的名片
A contracted carpenter in Queshi

永盛金铺在汕头市德安横街开张的广告。在动荡的年代，购买金银制品是最可靠的保值方法，在华洋杂处的汕头，传教士往往是金铺想要招徕的顾客

A jewelry store in Shantou, with missionaries being the potential clients

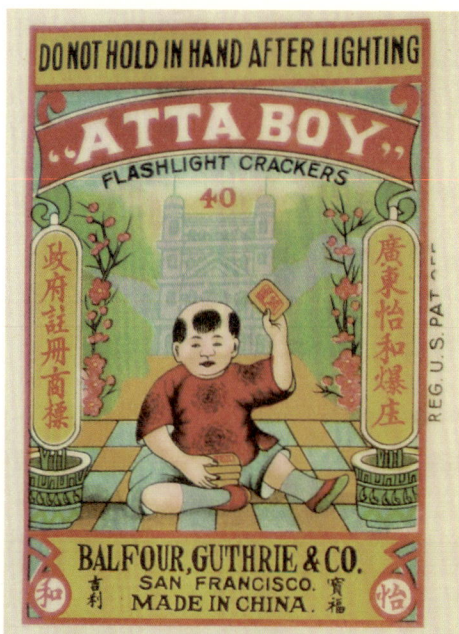

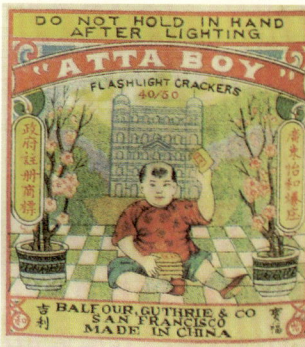

五彩缤纷的鞭炮包装纸
Beautiful wrapping paper for fire crackers

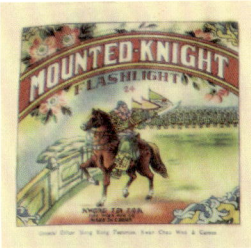

恭祝聖誕並賀年禧

信合公司鞠躬

Wishing you
a Merry Christmas
and
a Happy New Year
From
Sin Hah Co.,
SWATOW.

love to the Ashmores

恭祝聖誕並賀年禧

汕頭基督教青年會董幹事全部人敬祝

Wishing you
a Merry Christmas
and
o Happy New Year
From
Swatow Y. M. C. A.,
Swatow, South China.

1923.

恭祝聖誕並賀新禧

礐石中學青年會鞠躬

Wishing You a Merry Christmas
and
A Happy New Year
From
Y. M. C. A.
Swatow Academy

圣诞贺卡，它们代表了耶琳夫人
在汕头多年来积累的友情与回忆
**Christmas cards received by Lida
Scott Ashmore**

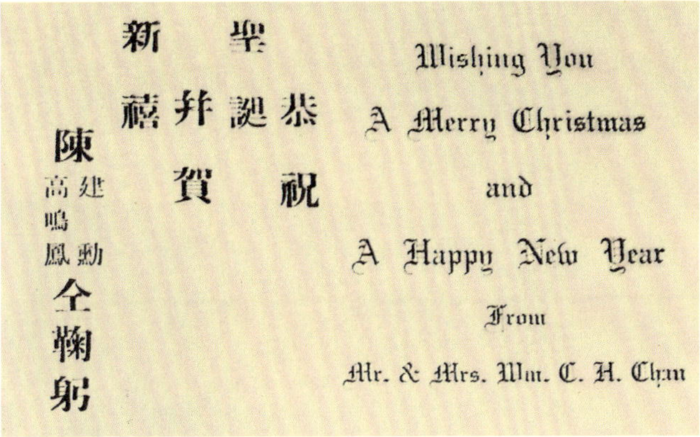

恭祝聖誕幷賀新禧

陳建勳高鳴鳳仝鞠躬

Wishing You
A Merry Christmas
and
A Happy New Year
From
Mr. & Mrs. Wm. C. H. Chan

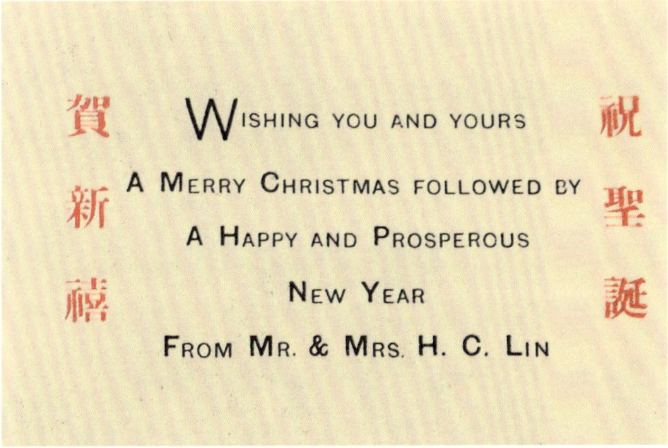

祝聖誕

賀新禧

WISHING YOU AND YOURS
A MERRY CHRISTMAS FOLLOWED BY
A HAPPY AND PROSPEROUS
NEW YEAR
FROM MR. & MRS. H. C. LIN

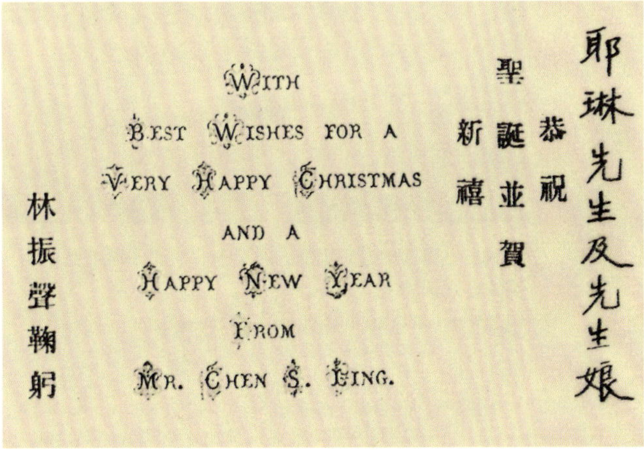

耶琳先生及先生娘

恭祝聖誕並賀新禧

林振聲鞠躬

WITH
BEST WISHES FOR A
VERY HAPPY CHRISTMAS
AND A
HAPPY NEW YEAR
FROM
MR. CHEN S. LING.

学童在圣诞树前进行表演，时至今日庆祝圣诞节已成为一种普遍的文娱活动

Children celebrated Christmas in the church